INNOVATIVE
SCHOOL DISCIPLINE

INNOVATIVE SCHOOL DISCIPLINE

By

JOHN MARTIN RICH, Ph.D.

The University of Texas at Austin

CHARLES C THOMAS • PUBLISHER
Springfield • Illinois • U.S.A.

Published and Distributed Throughout the World by
CHARLES C THOMAS • PUBLISHER
2600 South First Street
Springfield, Illinois 62717

© *1985 by* CHARLES C THOMAS • PUBLISHER

ISBN 0-398-05152-6

Library of Congress Catalog Card Number: 85-8052

Printed in the United States of America
Q-R-3

Library of Congress Cataloging in Publication Data

Rich, John Martin.
  Innovative school discipline.

  Bibliography: p.
  Includes Index.
  1. School discipline. I. Title.
LB3012.R55 1985   371.5   85-8052
ISBN 0-398-05152-6

PREFACE

DISCIPLINE was chosen by the public as the most significant problem in education in ten out of the last eleven Gallup polls. In a survey by the National Education Association of teacher attitudes, 54 percent said that student behavior interferes with their teaching. It is also a perennial problem and was probably of even greater concern to the American colonists.

The book's objectives are to place discipline in a broader and more meaningful context than the pressures of the moment and provide many useful innovative ideas. Disciplinary problems can be placed in a broader perspective by envisioning them in an historical and social context (chapter one). Also needed is a rationale for deciding which among the many contemporary models of discipline to adopt (chapter two). Teachers also should be acquainted with the latest research findings on topics related to discipline: educational policy, effective schools, classroom management, and the like (chapter five).

A further need is to study the disciplinary policies of innovative schools in order to understand what makes these programs successful. A questionnaire and follow-up interviews were used to gather this information, which is reported and assessed in chapters three and four. Finally, in chapter six the author presents his own theory of discipline as a possible alternative to the models offered in chapter two.

This book is intended for prospective teachers, teachers, school administrators, and teacher educators who are concerned about discipline problems. I would also be pleased if the book stimulated parents and others who work with youth to rethink the issues raised.

For suggestions about the questionnaire, I wish to thank my General Foundations of Education class, Ralph Cain, Jack Dunham, and John Laska. I am grateful to Laurie Miller for assistance in tallying the questionnaire, sitting in on some of the interviews, and many valuable observations. I received almost without exception much cooperation, courtesy, and consideration from the secondary school principals and other persons interviewed. Although there are too many people to list here, I am deeply grateful for their cooperation; many of them are mentioned by name in chapter four. I also thank those persons who completed and returned the questionnaire. Payne Thomas of Charles C Thomas Publisher offered encouragement by his conviction of the project's merit. And I warmly thank Gloria Zimmerman for her cheerful attitude, reliability, and excellent word processing skills.

CONTENTS

INNOVATIVE
SCHOOL DISCIPLINE

Chapter One

DISCIPLINARY PRACTICES
IN HISTORICAL PERSPECTIVE

DISCIPLINE has been consistently cited by the public as the most significant problem in education in Gallup polls of public attitudes toward education.[1] Some of the erosion of confidence in education could be ascribed to citizens' perceptions that schools have inadequately handled discipline. Administrators and teachers, though differing with one another and with the public about how to define and overcome this problem, are also seriously concerned about discipline. In a recent survey of teacher attitudes and practices, 54 percent said that student behavior interferes with their teaching.[2]

Many discipline books provide teachers with specific techniques for handling classroom disruptions and managing classrooms or offer administrators definite plans and proposals for reshaping the school environment to alleviate discipline problems. These materials vary widely in quality and scope.

What is still required are more powerful explanations that will get at the roots of disciplinary problems and thereby provide much needed understanding so that effective preventive measures can be initiated and healthier learning environments will ensue.

These tasks can be accomplished in several ways. Educators, first of all, need to see discipline in a broader perspective than the immediate pressures of specific daily problems. Instead, disciplinary problems can be envisioned as growing out of a larger social and cultural context, both historical and contemporary. In this way, promising programs and practices of past and present are assessed and placed in a balanced perspective; unsuccessful ones are identified and the reasons uncovered for their failures so that these mistakes will not likely be repeated.

A further need is to identify school systems that have introduced innovative and promising programs to determine the types of programs and their organization, and to discern how they are actually implemented. Case studies involving in-depth interviews help bring these data to life and offer essential insights. These findings are assessed in light of certain principles and the research literature. Finally, I present my own position and recommendations in terms of improving specific programs and practices.

In this first chapter, the topic of discipline will be placed in a broader historical perspective so that the reader can discern how the past has shaped our attitudes and thinking about discipline. Certain prevailing disciplinary models in American educational history are offered as representative of the programs and practice of the time; some of these models, as will be shown, still influence contemporary thought.

CALVINISTIC MODEL

Next to Martin Luther, John Calvin (1509-1564) was the most famous sixteenth century Protestant leader. Calvin acquired complete political power in Geneva, Switzerland by means of a constitution that made him ruler of the state and created a theocratic republic in which religion and politics were merged.

His *Institutes of Christian Religion* laid out his theology. Calvin claimed that God is omnipotent and omniscient and He knows the past, present, and future. This means that God also knows those who are to be saved and those who are to be eternally damned; in other words, God has foreknowledge and has predestined every person's fate. But Calvin also maintained that the outward sign of a person's election to grace is his moral behavior. Calvin and the elders spied upon citizens of Geneva to detect heretical and immoral acts, and some citizens were punished variously including banishment and execution; he was especially severe in punishing those who held religious views that differed from his own.

Calvinism spread widely: to the Huguenots in France, the Dutch Reformed Church in the Netherlands, and through the zealous preaching of John Knox in Scotland that led to the rise of Protestantism, and to the Puritans in the Massachusetts Bay Colony.

The Puritan religious outlook permeated much of the religious thinking of Americans for 150 years. The Puritans accepted the previously mentioned beliefs and also adopted Calvin's views of a wrathful God, original sin, obedience to God's commandments, obedience to the authority of parents and elders, and the value of hard work.

The New England Primer, which expressed Calvinistic teachings, was the famous little schoolbook that appeared in 1690 and lasted 125 years through many editions and various changes. The *Primer* exerted a great influence on the New England character, with its use in both church and school. A catechism in the *Primer* by John Cotton, a Boston minister and Protestant spokesman, titled "Spiritual Milk for American Babes . . .," asked the child:

Q. Are you then born Holy and Righteous?
A. No, my first parents sinned, and I in them.
Q. Are you then born a Sinner?
A. I was conceived in Sin and born in Iniquity.
Q. What is your Birth Sin?
A. Adam's Sin imputed to me, and a corrupt Nature dwelling in me.[3]

Jonathan's Edwards's orthodox Calvinism was expressed through the Congregational Church. Edwards declared: "That all are by nature the children of wrath, and heirs of hell; and they every one that has not been born again, whether he be young or old, is exposed every moment to eternal destruction, under the wrath of Almighty God. . ."[4] Edwards also observed that though children may seem to be innocent, they are not "if they are out of Christ, they are not so in God's sight, but are young vipers, and are in a most miserable condition, as well as grown persons; and they are naturally very senseless and stupid, being born as the wild ass's colt, and need much to awaken them."[5]

In Connecticut, the Governor and any two magistrates had the power to sentence any incorrigibles to hard labor and severe punishment in the house of correction.[6] In Massachusetts, any children above 16 years of age and of sufficient understanding who curses or smites their natural father or mother, shall be put to death, unless the parents have been "unchristianly negligent" in educating their children, or provoked them by extreme and cruel correction.[7]

In the Calvinistic belief in original sin, there was not much hope in religious and moral instruction other than placing one's complete faith in God's will and mercy. And because of predestination, some could not be saved despite their educational efforts. Nevertheless, it was expected in Massachusetts and Connecticut that children would recite catechisms. The child's obedience to parents and teachers was ordained by God. The child must obey their commands simply because they commanded it. By showing obedience to one's earthly father prepares one for obedience to one's heavenly Father. The pupil should be taught that school regulations are based on the office of the teacher. Moreover, severe punishment is not a last resort but "the first and the true remedy."[8]

In 1699, Cotton Mather wrote *A Family Well-Ordered* in which in the second part he vividly outlined the dreadful consequences that will befall the undutiful child. God's vengeful curse will lead him into worse sins and "will result in untimely and especially horrible deaths of hanging, suicide, and being eaten by vultures, and will result after death in eternal punishment in the utter darkness of Hell."[9]

In the Latin grammar school, the school day was long: beginning at six or seven in the morning, it would last until eleven o'clock; after two hours for lunch, it would resume and last until four or five o'clock. School continued through the summer, often six days a week. The boys would be expected to sit in rows of hard benches for long periods of time. Discipline was severe with emphasis on corporal punishment.

A boy was taught that time should never be wasted, that industry is a cardinal virtue and laziness an original sin; consequently, he must rise early and do chores before leaving for school and return home promptly after school for more work. He was expected to be diligent at school and show respect and obedience to teachers, parents, and guardians.

Much of the teacher's time was spent in maintaining order and inflicting punishment. An example of the arbitrariness of discipline is found in the following account of the Boston Latin grammar school in about the year 1802:

> The teacher told the class to write four lines. If, in looking around, he found anyone who had written his lines before the time was over, he thrashed him for writing too fast. If he had written none, he whipped him for laziness. When the copies were done, they all passed in procession with them through a narrow gangway, quite equivalent to running the gauntlet, as the teacher stood ready with a blow upon the utterance of a single word.[10]

REFORMIST ALTERNATIVES

Among the various objections to Calvinism, attacks were levelled at the doctrines of predestination and original sin. Predestination is inconsistent with moral responsibility and casts doubt upon God's powers and attributes. If God is omniscient, omnipotent, and all-benevolent (by definition), why does an all-benevolent God predestine humans to sin? Perhaps God does not know about all the sinning. But this would mean

God is not omniscient, which Calvin denies; therefore, God must not be all-benevolent because He willed some to sin and commit wicked acts against innocent human beings and against God's sacred laws. If human lives are predestined and God has full knowledge about sin and does not cause it, then God is not omnipotent and all-benevolent and there is no explanation for the sin, as human beings lack free will. Even if Calvin holds that in salvation divine grace renews the will, restoring freedom that was lost in original sin, this doctrine does not explain why God predestines some to sin. Thus, Calvinism is filled with many unresolved contradictions.

John Locke (1632-1704), English philosopher and political theorist, attacked the doctrine of innate ideas in 1687 and this, in turn, began to undermine the belief in original sin. As a physician in his observations of infants, he could not find any evidence of a precocious acquaintance with innate ideas.

One argument for innate ideas was universal assent to certain ideas. But Locke contended that if there were such universally held ideas, it would not prove them innate if there were any other way to show that people may reach universal agreement. However, he added, there are actually no ideas to which universal assent is given. Take certain logical laws: "whatever is, is;" and "it is impossible for the same thing to be, and not to be." These laws have been considered innate. But children and the mentally retarded have not the slightest apprehension or thought of them. It is unconvincing, he adds, to claim that these truths are imprinted upon the mind but are not perceived; since to say something is imprinted is to signify the truths are perceived.[11]

Locke declared that there are no innate ideas but that the mind at birth is a *tabula rasa*, a blank slate, on which experience writes. The origin of all ideas is experience, which is composed of sensation and reflection. If there is nothing innate in the human mind at birth, there can be no human depravity or original sin innate in the human heart. Since the mind is an empty capacity into which experiences can be poured, then all individuals are alike at birth; "all men are born equal."

Liberalizing views of the child also came from Anglicans, Quakers, minority religious sects, and from deistic and secular outlooks. By the middle of the nineteenth century, newer child-nature views began to emerge from Rousseauian romanticism, growing humanitarianism, and political conceptions of democracy, which claimed that the child needs greater liberty to prepare for citizenship responsibilities. Bronson Alcott, Samuel R. Hall, and Horace Mann proposed more temperate discipline policies.

Horace Mann (1796-1859), father of the common school, was instru-
mental in bringing about changes in disciplinary practices. In his untiring
efforts to gain public support for education in Massachusetts, Mann had
many occasions to observe undesirable practices. In a school of 250 pupils
that he visited, he reported that there had been 328 floggings in one
school week of five days.[12] Nevertheless, the public at this time was largely
in favor of such practices.

Mann recognized that although school discipline had been stern and
severe, the American Revolution and the adoption of the Constitution
ushered in a new era. Although these events did not change human nature, it put that nature in circumstances greatly different than it had ever
before experienced. The question is whether a more powerful public
agency can now help impart a higher moral tone to the public mind. One
of the greatest contributions schools can make is to educate students in
self-government. This means that students should understand the laws of
reason and duty before they will voluntarily comply with them.[13]

Mann noted that in the case of disobedient children, teachers must
first discipline their own feelings. They should act with the highest motives and recognize that love is a most potent corrective for those children
who have not been loved. Even wayward youth need to be treated kindly.
But the teacher should not expect too much from children right away.
One needs first to weaken the hold of undesirable principles and strengthen
desirable ones. This process can be aided by helping children avoid stiua-
tions where they have previously done wrong until the resolution to do the
right thing has been established. In addition, one should not issue commands unless it is certain that they will be obeyed. Thus the teacher
should not expect the child to act morally when selfish inclinations are
wrong. The temptation should be proportional to the ability to overcome
it, and therefore, the temptation is increased only when the power to re-
sist it is strengthened.[14]

Just as the physician takes pride in overcoming illness, says Mann, so
the teacher should not shrink from the toughest cases of stupidity and in-
corrigibleness. It is not that the teacher rejoices in the existence of wickedness; rather, where wickedness exists, the teacher is delighted to have the
opportunity to substitute strength for weakness and virtue for vice.
Teachers should not expel a vicious boy from school but expel vice from
the boy. Thus the teacher's ambition should be "to bring forward the lag-
ging and to reform the mischievous, to teach humility to the proud, and
benevolence to the cruel, and the love of duty to the sinful."[15]

Mann noted that although there is no necessary connection between literary competence, aptness to teach, and classroom management, a marked deficiency in any of the three areas renders the others of little value. The teacher must use considerable discretion in making assignments in order to avoid either overly short assignments that lead to idleness or overly heavy assignments that lead to mistakes and imperfections. Thus the lessons should be adapted to the student's capacities.[16]

It should be evident that Mann's views about discipline were a vast improvement over the harsh and cruel Calvinistic practices. By emphasizing student self-government and understanding, discussions of discipline were placed in a broader perspective and given a sense of direction. By seeing that the problems of discipline arise as well from teachers, who have undesirable traits or attitudes, marks an advance over exclusively blaming the child. This led to Mann's efforts that resulted in the establishment of a normal school in Lexington, Massachusetts, in 1839 for teacher preparation.

Despite the innovativeness of Mann's ideas about discipline, he did not develop a full-blown theory by which disciplinary programs that teachers and administrators could utilize in difficult cases. Nevertheless, Mann's humaneness, vision, and indefatigable efforts for public education were remarkable achievements. Five years after Mann resigned his post as secretary to the Massachusetts Board of Education, he became president of Antioch College. In his last address to the graduating class in 1859, the year of his death, he urged the graduates to heed his parting words: "Be ashamed to die until you have won some victory for humanity."

MILITARISTIC MODEL

Readers may be surprised to learn that at various times American education, in its organization and disciplinary practices, followed a military model. This model has not been restricted to the service academies and private military schools but extends to public schools, even though the military influences on the public school is less direct than on the service academies.

The two most fundamental archetypes of human society are the kinship community and the military community. Kinship, according to Nisbet, is found in guilds, churches, village communities, monasteries, and many other organizations concerned with tradition, religion, hierarchy, crafts, and learning.[19]

In contrast, the qualities of the military community are found in youth, mobility, secularism, discipline under command, and communism in military possessions. It often meant for youth an exciting escape from the boredom of ordinary peasant life; it was also a life of extraordinary danger and incessant discipline.[20]

Military discipline, according to Weber, uses emotional means of all sorts to gain devotion and to inspire; it is directed toward achieving a common cause. In place of charisma and devotion to a personal leader, military discipline substitutes "habituation to routinized skill." Thus the "content of discipline is nothing but the consistently rationalized, methodically trained and exact execution of the received order. . ."[21] Additionally, this conduct under orders is uniform and exhibits centralization of power.

But, one may wonder, what has all this to do with public education? Weber claims that "The discipline of the army gives birth to all discipline."[22] There is no direct historical link that connects the Pharaonic workshops and construction work, the Carthaginian Roman plantation, the mines of the late Middle Ages, the slave plantations of the colonies, and the modern factory. What they have in common is the element of discipline.

Military discipline is the ideal model for the modern capitalist factory, argues Weber. Organizational discipline in the factory is established on a rational basis. Using appropriate means of measurement, profitability is ascertained and, on these grounds, the American system of scientific management becomes an exemplar of rationality and calculation of work performances.[23] Among the organizations that adopted the military model of discipline, Nisbet observes, are the factories that replaced the guilds in postmedieval Europe, the prisons, the workhouses, the asylums, "and even the publicly operated schools."[24]

But where, then, can this militaristic discipline be found in public education? In a widely publicized national survey of American education in 1970, Silberman found that the most important characteristic that public schools share is their preoccupation with order and control. This characteristic is explained in part by the attempt to subordinate the individual to institutional objectives. Order and control are effected by adherence to a timetable, the requirement that students be silent, and the use of grades to rate, sort, and categorize students. The teacher-pupil relationship is a special form of dominance and subordination. Schools resemble "total institutions" like prisons, hospitals, and the armed services where one subgroup (the students) are committed to the institution and another subgroup (the staff) has greater freedom of movement, including the freedom to leave the institution entirely.[25]

Militaristic discipline, however, began much earlier in American education. The monitorial system, developed independently by Englishmen Joseph Lancaster and Andrew Bell, was adopted in America during the early nineteenth century. The system began in New York City in 1806, spread from Massachusetts to Georgia and as far west as Detroit; it declined in influence after 1830. Its objective was to provide mass education cheaply and efficiently; it was handled by having the teacher or master instruct monitors, who in turn instructed the boys under them. In a report on New York monitorial schools in 1828, the schools were commended because activity "keeps attention awake and interested, by permitting no moment of idleness or listlessness." Moreover, they were praised for their great saving of time and money, as masters in three schools taught 1,547 boys.[26]

The organization and even the language of the monitorial schools followed the militaristic model. The monitors were referred to as "youthful corporals of the teacher's regiment" who, after being taught a lesson from a printed card, took their "stations" about the wall and commenced teaching the other boys what they had learned. The instruction manual provided minutely detailed directions for organization, management, and teaching, and it forbade teachers from deviating from these instructions. Lancaster prescribed activity, emulation, order, and a type of military discipline.[27]

A primary means for imposing order and efficiency and developing the objectivity and efficiency of militaristic discipline was through the development of bureaucracies. The term refers to large organizations that are operated on the basis of efficiency in order to accomplish large-scale administrative tasks. The administrative hierarchy, the system of offices, and the rules and regulations governing their operation are deliberately contrived in order to achieve organizational goals.

The objectives of bureaucracy, according to Weber, are to eliminate irrational and emotional elements, to elevate precision, speed, continuity, unambiguity, and to encourage the subordination of personnel to the administrative hierarchy in order to minimize friction and reduce material and personnel costs. In a word, the objective of bureaucratic organizations is efficiency.

A number of measures are employed to promote efficiency. The offices are organized in a hierarchy so that each office is under the supervision and control of a higher one. Qualifications for each office are specified in writing, and the official functions to be performed are stipulated. The objective is to eliminate class privilege in appointments and to ensure that authority will be distributed on the basis of merit, not of wealth or influence. Employment is based on standards of competence that require specialized training. The hierarchical arrangement of offices provides a system of supervision used to evaluate performance, and the system of rules is designed to assure uniform performance of tasks.[28]

Katz has shown in a study that school bureaucracy emerged in Boston between 1850 and 1876. The reasons for this development were the increasing complexity of school administration, political influences in school operations, successful examples from industry of managing large work forces, and the aspirations and anxieties of school administrators.[29]

Bureaucracy grew in other ways: through an expanded growth of principals and supervisors, school district consolidation, and the emergence of a large and complex state education bureaucracy. Especially dramatic was the decline in school districts from their peak in 1932 of 127,529 to less than 16,000 nationwide today.

What does all of this mean for militaristic discipline? The vast bureaucratic machinery with its hierarchy of roles and status — not dissimilar to the armed forces — made school systems effective mechanisms for control through the application of uniform rules and sanctions. This meant that uniform standards of classroom management should be developed for all teachers in the system.

Bureaucratic leaders were incessantly in search of greater efficiencies in operation. Interest in the process of industrial management led to a number of studies in industry. Frederick W. Taylor advocated the scientific study of jobs based on time-studies of tasks, leading to the establishment of a standard time for each job and payment of wages in proportion to output.[30] Following Taylor's study, more systematic treatments dealt with the division of labor, specialization and departmentalization of functions, and managerial supervision.[31]

American businessmen, impressed with the principles of scientific management, pressured public education, from their positions of power on school boards, into adopting industrial management principles in the operation of school systems. The justification of such procedures was greater efficiency and economy. The scientific management approach, which prevailed in public education during the 1930s, viewed the teacher as the obedient servant to administrative authority.[32]

Other efficiency models can be found more recently. Accountability, the watchword of the 1970s, is a demand to judge schools by their outputs, to demonstrate a positive relationship between expenditures and desired results obtained. Accountability emphasizes measurement, efficiency, system models, and competitiveness. Efficient budgetary provisions and outputs in terms of performance on standardized achievement tests are the principal measures for determining quality.

In assessing the militaristic model, its advantages are the strong sense of order, control, and authority it brought into education. Teachers knew more precisely what was expected of them and perceived that administrators would reward orderly classrooms where rules are strictly observed. Bureaucracies were, in some cases, more efficient and fairer than the organizational forms they superseded. They were fairer because they largely eliminated political pressure and outside influences in hiring and promotion.

But bureaucracies have been correctly perceived in some cases as top-heavy organizations filled with "red tape," slavish and unimaginative bureaucrats, large-scale inefficiencies, breakdowns in effective communication between the line and staff, and a tendency to alienate some teachers and students. The pervasive sense of "joylessness" that Silberman found in his observations of schools he attributed to the bureaucratic system of control and a loss of meaning and purpose.

The militaristic model confuses control with discipline. Control may be gained by coercion, the use of drugs, tranquilizers, conditioning, threats, and related measures. But this is not discipline if what is involved in discipline is student agency; that is, positive activity on the part of students to bring about desirable ends. This is not to say that under exceptional conditions when disruptions cannot be handled that teachers would not resort to control measures: they would do so but usually only temporarily (especially with effective teachers) until more positive measures could be successfully initiated. The point that needs to be underscored is that control is not an *end* (as the militaristic model would claim) but at best a temporary *means* until more desirable practices can be instituted. Moreover, control measures that dehumanize students, fail to respect them as persons, and deny them their rights should be prohibited. Unfortunately, too many controls infringe in these areas; thus, it may be helpful to use other early disciplinary models that offer greater promise.

The militaristic model makes not only control but order an end, not a means to an end. Of course, some degree of orderliness is needed in all organizations or they would eventually be unable to function. But orderliness and control are at best means, and not always the most desirable means, for facilitating the achievement of educational goals. Moreover, not all forms of order are desirable, as there usually is a great deal of order in a concentration camp. Educators must ascertain that the measures used for maintaining order are not unethical and/or dehumanizing. It would be better to have more disorder rather than employ such measures; fortunately, alternatives to such practices are readily available, as will be shown in this and subsequent chapters.

Finally, the militaristic model has an overly restricted conception of authority relationships. Authority is conceived as unquestioning obedience to one's superior in the hierarchy — the student's unquestioning obedience to the teacher, the teacher to the administration. In other words, the relationship is largely authoritarian. But there are various types of authority, which means that authority serves different forms and functions. Authority can take the form of expert, counselor, model, legislator, disciplinarian, and office holder.[33] The point is that the militaristic model of authority is unidimensional and rigid, thereby impoverishing interpersonal relations in schools.

THE ESSENTIALIST MODEL

The essentialist tradition emphasizes the value of transmitting the cultural heritage to all youth, of seeing that they are soundly trained in "the fundamentals," and that they study the basic disciplines. Subjects should be studied in terms of a logical, chronological, or causal approach rather than organized along the lines of activities and projects based on the immediate needs of students (as progressives had done). Only in this way will students develop a sound grasp and appreciation of the heritage, and only in a curriculum that stresses these elements will they develop their minds, become educated persons, and exhibit good citizenship practices.

In order to develop these objectives, students cannot always study what strikes their immediate interests, but must study what they need in order to fulfill their adult responsibilities. And in reacting to the considerable freedom given students in progressive classrooms, essentialists contend that discipline is no longer being stressed, resulting in a failure to develop strong study habits and an adequate mastery of the fundamental disciplines.

A number of essentialists have forcefully expressed their ideas about discipline. Demiashkevich defines discipline as an ensemble of rules and regulations governing student behavior. The purpose of discipline is ultimately self-discipline, and school discipline can greatly contribute to sound moral habits. But there are wrong and right kinds of discipline: the wrong kind breaks the spirit and leads to unquestionable obedience; whereas the right kind is designed to form good moral habits. Thus it is important that students be made to see the significance of school rules and regulations so that they will accept them. Punishment is not in itself objectionable; therefore, when exhortations have been applied but prove useless, the teacher may resort to punishment.[34]

Harris notes four cardinal duties in the schoolroom: regularity, punctuality, silence, and industry. These duties extend beyond the school to the development of good character in everyday life. The pupil should become conscious of responsibility in the act of obedience to a higher will. This responsibility implies a sense of freedom as the child becomes cognizant of the ability to obey or disobey. The child needs to learn responsibility not only for positive acts but for the neglect of duties, to learn that it is he and not his environment that is responsible for what is done or left undone.[35]

Other essentialists talk about the importance of social control. Finney claims that too much emphasis has been placed on individual initiative and independence as a reult of misconceptions about democracy. He sees nothing wrong with drill and memorization; in fact, there may be occasions where regimentation is needed. Resistance from the young should be expected because of the conflict between youthful instincts and social demands; yet social stability requires that resistance be overcome. Being indulgent with children is not in their own interest, for the alternative to control is not freedom but social chaos.[36]

Essentialists strenuously object to progressives catering to the child's interests. Hocking insists that without difficulty, no lasting interest is possible. In other words, interest accompanies a task that is based on mental momentum or mental effort. One gains interest in working with materials of increased difficulty, which at first may discourage pupils and drive out interest until sufficient mastery is gained.[37] Reflecting similar views, Horne states that the opposite of interest is not hard work but drudgery. Interest is a feeling we have in something or some activity; it is not entertainment of pupils, but attainment by the pupils; it is not play, but attractive and compelling work. There must be discipline in doing what is necessary even if it is disagreeable; such efforts may lead to discipline; yet even if it does not do so, the obligatory task must still be done. Thus pupils will learn to do their duties.

A related view of discipline and the unruly school is offered by Bagley. Some pupils, he says, spend much time trying to cause trouble; therefore, in order to change this behavior, the pupils must feel the compelling force

of work and the responsibility of the social group. This means that the pupil's peers must take some responsibility for supervising each individual's
conduct. The qualitative standards of work must also be raised by use of
objective scales, encouraging collective or group competition.[39] More recent essentialists tend to agree with the earlier essentialist views expressed
above and have not advanced a new position on discipline.[40]

In conclusion, essentialism at its best provides structure, order, and a
clear sense of responsibility in both the learning process and interpersonal
relations; at its worst, it resembles a diluted Calvinism without the theo-
logical baggage. Obviously no class instruction can take place without
some order and cooperation from students, and learning is impossible
without some discipline, whether in the form of organized and directed
thinking or in various self-management skills. Essentialists have also
highlighted the dangers of catering exclusively to the child's interests and
failing to encourage sound work and study habits. Responsibility has
been placed on the student's shoulders rather than make the teacher the
blame for much student misbehavior and learning failures.

Despite these strengths, essentialist discipline makes the teacher an
authority figure who at times becomes authoritarian. The relation between teacher and pupil is unilateral, with the teacher giving instructions
and the pupils following orders. The opportunity for the young to eventually become reflective thinkers and more autonomous persons becomes
threatened if the model is imposed too literally. Moreover, although essentialists tell us that much effort is needed to gain knowledge, they tend to
neglect the improvement of instruction and better planning by the teacher
as a means for improving discipline and making learning tasks less ardu-
ous and more of a delight than a chore. Additionally, essentialists need to
relate their recommendations more closely to what is known about human development and what could reasonably be expected of the child at
different stages of development. Whatever the reader's opinion of the essentialist model, it should be noted that it has once again become influential in the 1980s in terms of the back-to-basics movement and the
movement's proliferation of fundamental schools.

THE PROGRESSIVE MODEL

The model most objected to by essentialists is the progressive model.
Progressive education was both a movement and a philosophy that came
to fruition in the United States during the early part of this century. Its

ideas also had some influence in Europe, Australia, and other parts of the world. The progressives sought to bring the child center-stage, to focus on the child's needs and interests and to develop the whole child.

Progressivism was in part a reaction to more traditional educational practices such as essentialism. Essentialists had concerned themselves with cognitive development of the student through imparting the cultural heritage in a subject curriculum. The curriculum was defined in advance without teacher-pupil planning; it was assumed that there are certain things that should be learned whether or not the child was interested in learning them. Progressives objected, stating that the child's needs and interests, not subject-matter laid out in advance, should be the focus of the teacher's attention. Needs and interests could be assessed by carefully observing and questioning students in class and by examining research findings about human growth and development.

This perspective led progressives to deviate sharply from the subject curriculum by developing innovative plans that they believed would be more carefully attuned to children's interests and the ways that they learn best. Among the new curricular patterns tested were the broad fields curriculum, experience curriculum, life functions, core curriculum, and others.

The child has innumerable interests upon which the teacher could capitalize to promote learning; it only seemed that the child's interests were constricted because traditional schools had suppressed these interests by forcing subjects to be learned that had little or no connecting links to the child's life.

Progressives greatly enlarged the curriculum's scope to fully recognize not only interests and needs but to give full attention to the "whole child." This meant that the school's responsibility is not only intellectual development, but provisions must be made for social, emotional, moral, and physical development; moreover, if the school was church-supported, spiritual development could be included.

Completely rejecting Calvinism and its stern disciplinary policies, progressives accepted Rousseau's dictum that the child is born basically good. This meant that it no longer was necessary to impose upon the child stringent rules and regulations and exact harsh punishment for disobedience. Instead, the child could be permitted to develop naturally, to explore and create.

To carry out these changes, the teacher could no longer be an authority figure and an unyielding disciplinarian and taskmaster; rather, the teacher's role became a facilitator of learning, one who arranged stimulating learning environments for students and worked with them individually and in groups. "The good teacher is now the one who puts friendliness in place of authority, who secures enthusiasm in place of mere obedience."[41]   Thus children are not governed by fear of teacher disapproval but are "happily busy." As a substitution for military discipline and competition, cooperation was substituted where the student subordinated herself for larger goals considered worthwhile.[42] Since schools are preparing youth for democratic life, it should be recognized, according to the Cardinal Principles of Education, that democacy sanctions neither the exploitation of citizens by society, nor the society's interests by individuals. "The purpose of democracy," the commission report adds, "is to organize society so that each member may develop his personality primarily through activities designed for the well-being of his fellow members and of society as a whole."[43]

Most progressives were child-centered. Rugg and Shumaker proclaimed that in the activity school, children will be free from rigid schedules, coercion, and lock-step methods; children will be active and engaged in self-expression; they will not study subjects but real life interactions. Children no longer will be passive or merely responsive to what is being taught, but will learn how to learn by themselves. The teacher no longer has to worry about discipline because the child becomes self-directed, self-disciplined. The activity or child-centered schools have eradicated the concept of discipline and implanted the concept of growth.[44]

A. S. Neill (1883-1973) founded and directed Summerhill, a private school in England that became one of the world's most famous free schools. Neill began writing about his ideas in the 1920s, but it was not until the early 1960s that his books became widely read in the United States; by the late 1960s, his books influenced the free school movement in this country.

Utilizing play, children's own interest and creativity, their capacity to work and live with their peers in a cooperative arrangement by means of developing their own rules and regulations and seeing that they are enforced, form the basis of Summerhill. The impact of Neill's personality and the ability to convey his ideas to a growing audience is in large part responsible for Summerhill's renown.

In working with problem children, Neill concluded that neurosis is implanted by early moral instruction. He found that parents exhorted children to live up to certain ideals (hard work, cleanliness, being good) and that these ideals ran into conflict with children's interests and habits. These ideals were reinforced by prohibitions and the use of such words as "dirty" and "naughty" that were buttressed by threats of punishment and emotional bribery ("Mother won't love you if you do that"). The most harmful application of this instruction, Neill believed, is in terms of sex. This type of discipline creates a tension between the child's interest in the forbidden activity and the guilt created by yielding to temptation. This in turn led to a neurosis, anti-social behavior, or general nervousness and unhappiness. But Neill also claimed that childhood nervousness stems from a lack of love and affection.

In dealing with children who had failed to receive love and approval, it is important, he believes, to take their point of view and not try to channel them toward certain ends, which the child would only associate with disapproving adults. Neill tried several measures to combat childhood neurosis: sublimation, direct analysis to uncover the roots of the neurosis, and the development of an accepting permissive environment.

If a child threw mud on a door that Neill had just painted, Neill would swear at him; but if the child had done this act after just transferring from a hateful school, Neill would help the child sling mud so the child could get back at authority. Neill insisted that he observed a distinction in his policies between liberty and license: that license may be necessary for a cure, but ordinary children should respect others' rights.[45]

Neill established a system of self-government at Summerhill. He retained responsibility for overall administrative matters, diet and health, but turned over the rest of the operations to students, who met weekly to discuss rules and to determine action to be taken against violators. Everyone was encouraged to express their views, and each student older than eight had one vote. Neill claimed that self-government is good civic education; it is therapeutic because it releases tensions; children are more likely to abide by rules that they, rather than adults, make; and since peers impose punishment, better relations are promoted between teachers and students because the teacher is no longer a disciplinarian.[46]

In assessing the progressive model, it should be evident that the child was given more attention than in previous models, and a serious attempt was made to meet the child's needs and interests. Discipline was more closely related to instruction and the social life of the school. By connecting learning activities to the child's interests, there was less likelihood that the child would misbehave; and by drawing upon peers to develop and enforce rules, the teacher's role was transformed to a facilitator of learning. By enlarging the curriculum to take care of the whole child, student interests and needs would more likely be fulfilled and therefore disruptions might be reduced.

One problem with the progressive model is its permissiveness. Following Rousseau, it assumes that the child is basically good and that a laissez-faire approach where the child is afforded maximum freedom within some constraints is the best policy. Permissiveness was not always what it purported to be, however. When children, left to their own devices, did not arrive at rules or decisions that teachers considered desirable, such progressive practices sometimes were cast aside in order to subtly coerce children to accept the "right" decisions. A more serious problem with permissiveness is that it is based on a faulty notion of children's capacities to make wise decisions by overlooking the child's inexperience in worldly affairs, immaturity, limited cognitive development, and lower-order moral reasoning.

Certain types of child-rearing conditions support the development of autonomy. Parental warmth and concern, a democratic atmosphere, and consideration and consistency in rule enforcement are supportive conditions.[47] Autocratic or very lenient parents usually have children who are low in self-confidence and either dependent or rebellious.[48]

The progressives also overestimate the child's ability to use a discovery approach in gaining basic knowledge and understanding. The emphasis on discovery and self-expression stems not only from a belief that the child learns best by this approach, but also arises from fear that the teacher will become autocratic by imposing her will on the child. The use of an experience curriculum where the child must initiate learning and gain knowledge first-hand may be a welcome change from lectures and expository presentations but, when used exclusively, could be fallacious and dangerous. It assumes that the immature child should learn from scratch what it has taken civilizations thousands of years to discover, develop, and refine. There are simply not enough lifetimes for any student to discover knowledge experientially; it is necessary instead to mix expository learning with experiential learning.

Let us assume that the child is left to discover through experience a moral code. How would this be done? Without being shown by adults, the child would not know what it meant to follow a rule; and without being able to follow rules, the child could not develop a morality and eventually become an independent moral agent where she understands how to follow her own rules. Moral rules have to be learned despite counterinclinations to act on impulse or do whatever makes one feel good, if only momentarily, irrespective of how it affects others. Thus adults will need to teach children to follow rules, reinforce desirable behavior, and establish worthy models for children to emulate.

THE PRAGMATIC MODEL

John Dewey (1859-1952), generally considered America's leading educational philosopher during the first half of this century, was considered a pragmatist and a progressive. Yet he was not child-centered and criticized this branch of progressivism for alleged excesses and failure to build a defensible philosophy of education.

Pragmatism holds that ideas must be referred to their consequences for their truth and meaning. Ideas become instruments for solving problems, attaining goals, and anticipating future experiences.

Discipline, according to Dewey, has been conceived by one theory as the application of external constraints and by another theory as an absence of restraint in the name of freedom. (Although he does not name these theories, evidently they are, respectively, versions of essentialism and progressivism.) The first theory, he claims, leads to drill and external modes of action that caused studies to be disagreeable; the second theory leads to immediate expression and impulse, which fails to promote reflective thinking.

Discipline, instead, is positive and constructive. It provides control over the means necessary to achieve ends and the ability to value and test ends. A painter is disciplined to the extent that he can use his materials and can exhibit vision and imagination. Genuine freedom is intellectual: it rests in the power of thought.[49] One is free to the extent of acting in harmony with the knowledge one possesses; freedom implies an understanding and mastery of the situation.[50] Thus the progressives were correct that the student should be freed from autocratic and arbitrary constraints; however, they did not go far enough, as the student must also be free to deal with meaningful problem-solving activities.

Another reason Dewey could not accept the child-centered progressives' laissez-faire conception of freedom was his belief that each individual is a social individual, and that society is "an organic union of individuals." He viewed the school as "a mode of social life," a place where one gains moral training by having to learn to relate to others.[51] For Dewey, the school can become "a miniature community, an embryonic society." School life organizes itself on a social basis, and the principle of school discipline or order is found within this organization. Order is relative to an end; therefore if the end is the development of social cooperation and community life, discipline must grow out of these conditions and be relative to it (not an end in itself).[52] Thus what is sought is a freedom which is power: an ability to develop purposes, judge wisely, and evaluate desires by the consequences of acting upon them.[53]

A person is disciplined, according to Dewey, who is trained to consider his actions and undertake them deliberately. In addition, the person has the ability to endure distractions and difficulties. "Discipline means power at command; mastery of the resources available for carrying through the action undertaken."[54] But Dewey notes that discipline is too often associated with the use of will power to study what one does not like, a negative view, rather than conceiving discipline in terms of growth in ability and achievement.

Dewey sought to improve the quality of educative experiences. By education, he meant that "reconstruction or reorganization of experience which adds to the meaning of experience, and which increases ability to direct the course of subsequent experience."[55] He urged that our range of outlook be enlarged. "What the best and wisest parent wants for his own child, that must the community want for all of its children."[56]

In appraising Dewey's views of discipline, he advanced educational thought by showing that there are weaknesses in both essentialist and progressive views of freedom and discipline and by substituting his own approach. Dewey was able to place discipline within contexts in which persons seek to solve problems and gain greater control of their environment; discipline and order become *means* rather than *ends* for the resolution of meaningful problems and the growth in ability to deal effectively with subsequent problems. He associated genuine freedom not merely with an absence of restraint but with the power of thought and intelligent action.

Obvious criticisms of Dewey's position would come from all of the previous models presented. Less obvious would be weaknesses in the notion of the school as a miniature community and the development of discipline within social cooperative activities in the life of the school. Since the period when Dewey developed these ideas, criticisms have been made of the socialization function of the school. These criticisms claim that through various socialization practices schools become coercive institutions that exact conformity and obedience to a set of white middle class values that prepare graduates to take their place as docile workers in the capitalistic industrial economy. Although it is true that Dewey always sought to develop reflective individuals, he was not fully cognizant that the social cooperation practices he advocated could be subverted for undesirable ends. Additionally, the school as a miniature community concept, including Dewey's emphasis on children studying occupations, may tend to transmit both desirable and undesirable practices of the larger society; hence, what is needed is the construction of more ideal models to pursue.

Another type of criticism would emanate from advocates of punishment and conditioning. They would fault Dewey for not recognizing that the young child is unprepared to engage in the independent reflective thinking that Dewey extols but needs instead punishment to prevent wrongdoing and to prevent harm, or needs a system based on simple stimulus-response patterns where the child is rewarded immediately for desirable behavior. In other words, Dewey is appealing to higher cognitive processes but the child lacks sufficient intellectual maturity to profit from this approach. This criticism, however, is only partly valid because resourceful teachers could adopt Dewey's model so that it relates to the way that children of different ages think. Thus we have a case of conflicting models, and in the next chapter many of these newer models will be presented.

NOTES

1. George H. Gallup, "The 16th Annual Poll of the Public's Attitudes Toward the Public Schools," *Phi Delta Kappan* 66 (September 1984):23-28.
2. "NEA Survey Investigates Teacher Attitudes, Practices," *Phi Delta Kappan* 62 (September 1980):49.
3. "The New England Primer,," in *Readings in Public Education in the United States*, ed. Ellwood P. Cubberley (New York: Houghton Mifflin, 1934), p. 51.
4. "Jonathan Edwards Describes the 'Children of Wrath,'" in *Education in the United States: A Documentary History*, Vol. I, ed. Sol Cohen (New York: Random House, 1974), p. 478.
5. Ibid.
6. "Instructions for the Punishment of Incorrigible Children in Connecticut (1642)," ibid., p. 370.
7. "Instructions for the Punishment of Incorrigible Children in Connecticut (1642)," ibid., pp. 370-371.
8. Pickens E. Harris, *Changing Conceptions of School Discipline* (New York: Macmillan, 1928), p. 79.
9. R. Freeman Butts and Lawrence A. Cremin, *A History of Education in American Culture* (New York: Holt, 1953), p. 69.
10. Harris, *Changing Conceptions*, p. 18.
11. John Locke, *An Essay Concerning Human Understanding*, Bk. I, Ch. 2.
12. John S. Brubacher, *A History of the Problems of Education* (New York: McGraw-Hill, 1947), p. 229.
13. Horace Mann, "Ninth Annual Report (1945)," in *The Republic and the School: Horace Mann on the Education of Free Men*, ed. Lawrence A. Cremin (New York: Bureau of Publications, Teachers College, Columbia University, 1957), pp. 57-59).

14. Louis Filler, ed., *Horace Mann on the Crisis in Education* (Yellow Springs, Ohio: Antioch Press, 1965), pp. 148-152.
15. Ibid., p. 191.
16. Mann, "Fourth Annual Report," in *Republic and the School*, pp. 48-52.
17. Ibid., p. 50.
18. Harris, *Changing Conceptions*, pp. 60-85.
19. Robert Nisbet, *The Social Philosophers* (London: Paladin, 1976), pp.36-37.
20. Ibid., p. 62.
21. "The Meaning of Discipline." In H. H. Gerth and C. Wright Mills, *From Max Weber: Essays in Sociology* (New York: Oxford University Press, 1958), p. 254.
22. Ibid., p. 261.
23. Ibid.
24. Nisbet, *Social Philosophers*, p. 37.
25. Charles E. Silberman, *Crisis in the Classroom* (New York: Random House, 1970), pp. 122-123, 130, 146.
26. "Report of the New Yok Lancastrian Schools" in *Readings*, pp. 137-138.
27. Ellwood P. Cubberley, *Public Education in the United States*, rev. ed. (Boston: Houghton Mifflin, 1947), pp. 128-134.
28. *From Max Weber*, ch. 8; Max Weber, *The Theory of Social and Economic Organization*, trans. A. M. Henderson and Talcott Parsons (New York: Free Press, 1957).
29. Michael B. Katz, *Class, Bureaucracy, and Schools: The Illusion of Educational Change in America*, Expanded Ed. (New York: Free Press, 1957).
30. Frederick W. Taylor, *Scientific Management* (New York: Harper, 1911).
31. James D. Monney and Alan C. Reiley, *Onward Industry* (New York: Harper, 1931).
32. Raymond E. Callahan, *Education and the Cult of Efficiency* (Chicago: University of Chicago Press, 1962).
33. See my *Discipline and Authority in School and Family* (Lexington, Mass.: Lexington Books, 1982), pp. 9-19.
34. Michael Demiashkevich, *An Introduction to the Philosophy of Education* (New York: American Book Co., 1935), pp. 306-313.
35. W. T. Harris, "School Discipline," in *The Third Yearbook of the National Herbart Society* (Chicago: University of Chicago Press, 1908), pp. 65-66.
36. Ross L. Finney, *A Sociological Philosophy of Education* (New York: Macmillan, 1928), pp. 469-470.
37. William E. Hocking, *Human Nature and Its Remaking* (New Haven, Conn.: Yale University Press, 1929), p. 271.
38. Herman H. Horne, *The Philosophy of Education* (New York: Macmillan, 1927), pp. 189-191, 312-314.
39. William Chandler Bagely, *School Discipline* (New York: Macmillan, 1914), ch. 5.
40. See: Mortimer Smith, *And Madly Teach* (Chicago: Henry Regnery, 1949); B. I. Bell, *Crisis in Education* (New York: Whittlesey House, 1949); and H. G. Rickover, *American Education — A National Failure* (New York: E. P. Dutton, 1963).
41. Morton Snyder, "What is Progressive Education?" in *Readings*, p. 420.
42. A. Flexner and F. P. Bachman, "Merits of the Gary Plan," ibid., p. 418.
43. "The Seven Cardinal Principles of Secondary Education, 1918." in *The American Legacy of Learning*, eds. J. H. Best and R. T. Sidwell (Philadelphia: Lippincott, 1967), pp. 273-274.

44. Harold Rugg and Ann Shumaker, *The Child-Centered School* (New York: World Book Co., 1928), pp. 102, 314.

45. A. S. Neill, *The Problem Child* (New York: Hermitage Press, 1949); and *The Problem Teacher* (New York: International University Press, 1944).

46. A. S. Neill, *Summerhill: A Radical Approach to Child Rearing* (New York: Hart, 1960).

47. U. Bronfenbrenner, "Some Family Antecedents of Responsibility and Leadership in Adolescents." in *Leadership and Interpersonal Behavior*, eds. L. Petrullo and B. Bass (New York: Holt, Rinehart and Winston, 1961), pp. 239-271.

48. E. Douvan and J. Adelson, *The Adolescent Experience* (New York: Wile, 1966); and G. H. Elder, "Structural Variations in the Child Rearing Relationship," *Sociometry* 25 (1962):241-262.

49. John Dewey, *How We Think* (New York: Heath, 1933), pp. 85-90.

50. John Dewey, *The Quest for Certainty* (New York: Henry Holt, 1927), p. 249f.

51. "My Pedagogic Creed," in *John Dewey on Education: Selected Writings*, ed. R. D. Archambault (New York: Modern Library, 1964), pp. 429-431.

52. "The School and Society," ibid., pp. 301-303.

53. John Dewey, *Experience and Education* (New York: Collier Books, 1963), pp. 63-64.

54. John Dewey, *Democracy and Education* (New York: Free Press, 1944), p. 129.

55. Ibid., p. 76.

56. "The School and Society," p. 295.

Chapter Two

CONTEMPORARY DISCIPLINARY VIEWPOINTS

THIS CHAPTER will review selected disciplinary systems of contemporary authors that represent various schools of thought. These positions will not be repetitious of chapter one because some important new theories and ideas have emerged in recent decades. Readers can thereby assess their own views more fully and see where they stand in relation to each of these recent systems.

Selections are based not only on the writer's influence but also on the need to provide distinctive models and a full range of contemporary positions. Systems of discipline presented are Kohl's Natural Development Model, Gordon's Teacher Effectiveness Training, Altschuler's Social Literacy Approach, Glasser's Deficiency Model, Dreikur's Social Consequences, Skinner and Behavior Modification, and Canter's Assertive Discipline.

KOHL'S NATURAL DEVELOPMENT MODEL

Herbert Kohl has written widely and received considerable attention for his ideas about working with children and youth. As a former teacher in Harlem, he was involved with parents in the struggle for community control of schools, and was director of the Teachers and Writers Collaborative at the Horace Mann Lincoln Institute of School Experimentation. After serving as a director of an experimental program in Berkeley, California schools, he is now teaching kindergarten and first grade there.

Kohl is committed to open education and child-centered learning. What is important, he believes, is to discover the student's needs and build a learning environment that emerges from these needs and fosters them. In other words, the teacher must be responsive to the way students naturally grow and develop.

26

For Kohl the emphasis is on observing, listening and understanding the young so that a flexible and suitable environment can be created. "Openness, naturalness, and closeness," along with "consistency and strength," are necessary traits in working with youngsters, even though, admittedly, they are difficult to develop.[1] Personal problems should not be used as an excuse for abandoning students or expecting them to handle problems that adults may not handle well. Though it may be threatening to some teachers, students should be treated as "moral equals" in the sense that the same rules apply to both. The open teacher does not bully but is responsive to criticism and changes behavior whenever the criticism is sound.[2] The teacher should also have the strength to admit failure.[3]

Not only the teacher-student relations are important but the total classroom as well; therefore he insists that the teacher should not hesitate to modify classroom arrangements and timetables. Since privacy, Kohl believes, is necessary for student development, classroom furniture can be arranged to ensure greater privacy. Private places are needed for both small-group work and solitary places for thought. The privacy can be built into classrooms by using fabrics, rug dividers, clothing closets, and the like.

Regulations should be reviewed by teachers to be sure that they are necessary and do not squelch students. Why should students line up the same way every day, raise their hands, and not talk to each other? The open classroom teacher has to relinquish some power; doing so, however, need not result in permissiveness, for the teacher should express feelings forthrightly about student behavior and teacher concerns.

The teacher's objective is to create an environment in which trust and responsibility can evolve.[4] Each teacher must determine to what extent the school system will permit an open classroom. Compromises are necessary in order to survive; but survival in some schools is undesirable, Kohl insists, and therefore it is better to resign or be terminated.

Students should not be permitted to bully or injure another, injure or maim themselves, interfere or prevent others from working, or destroy another student's work or classroom materials. Ideally the entire class should see that these rules are enforced; above all, the teacher must enforce them. Sooner or later each open classroom student will attempt to test these limits; it is the teacher's task to respect the student's strength while consistently enforcing these limits. When a discipline problem arises that concerns the entire class, the best way to handle it is by using a fable or story that can be discussed without anyone being embarrassed.

Thus for Kohl, discipline evolves out of open-classroom interaction fostered by the teacher's naturalness, consistency, and strength, traits that do not resort to numerous rules but rely on establishing outer limits beyond which student welfare and growth would be endangered.

In assessing Kohl's approach, it provides a flexible, open-classroom setting in which the teacher displays such positive traits as responsiveness, naturalness, openness, closeness, and toughness. The teacher observes natural development and attempts to provide an environment that will best nurture it. A humane environment is constructed in which much freedom is available to learn, explore, and create. Especially under Kohl's guidance, students will likely find it a happy atmosphere and will usually enjoy their school experiences. Discipline becomes a natural outgrowth of such a healthy learning environment.

But the natural development model exhibits a number of weaknesses. By providing an atmosphere for natural development and with few disciplinary limits, it is still not evident where the teacher will end up by following the sequences of development stages as they unfold. Moreover, as some potentials develop they conflict with others and some criteria are needed for adjudicating the conflict. The teacher needs to make critical decisions about which growth tendencies to promote and which to be curbed. Growth itself exhibits and sets limits on what the child can do; it does not prescribe, however. Needed direction is not provided by Kohl's nebulous statement that "the main goal of schooling is to enable young people to get out of school able to do something they value and can give to others."[6]

Student interests play a large role in determining Kohl's curriculum. But such interests cannot determine content because sudents have interests that are educationally undesirable and there are things which they need to learn in which interest may be absent. The task is that of taking sporadic and fitful interests and broadening and deepening them in those activities in which they ought to become interested. Although Kohl attempts to do this to some extent, he still views the curriculum as emerging out of student interests.

Kohl's role for teachers is difficult for many teachers to emulate because it requires an open classroom where the teacher is expected to manifest "consistency," "strength," "naturalness," and "closeness" in a relationship of moral equality. Most teachers prefer a more structured classroom environment wherein teacher-student relations are more sharply delineated. Until there are more successful programs to prepare teachers for open classrooms, Kohl's type of teacher will be in a minority.

GORDON'S TEACHER EFFECTIVENESS TRAINING

Thomas Gordon's approach to teacher effectiveness training originated from his attempts to help parents deal effectively with their children. The theoretical underpinnings are drawn from Carl Rogers' client-centered therapy in which the counselor takes an empathic, nonjudgmental position. Rogers held that the therapist should not impose solutions but should create "positive regard" whereby the client can overcome a lack of self-esteem, which is usually the source of the problem rather than from an illness that needs the medical model of psychiatry.

Gordon devotes much time to helping teachers communicate more effectively with students. Communication, for Gordon, is to help persons understand what others are saying and to learn to formulate responsive messages that promote mutual understanding. The teacher's first step is to look critically at a disruptive student to let the student know that the teacher is aware of what he is doing, that the teacher has trust in the student's ability of self-correction, and that the teacher is available should help be needed. The teacher's critical listening in silence encourages the student to share concerns with the teacher.

Sometimes students have trouble in initiating a statement or hesitate after getting started. The teacher can use "door openers" or "reopeners" that provide additional encouragement (e.g.: "Would you like to say more about that?" or "I'm interested in what you are saying."). These are open-ended questions or statements that contain no evaluation about what is said. The teacher avoids "roadblocks" that inhibit or stop communication; these roadblocks include ordering, threatening, moralizing, advising, lecturing, and giving logical arguments. They also include judging, blaming, labeling, interpreting, analyzing, diagnosing, praising, sympathizing, interrogating, being sarcastic, and humoring. Gordon believes the roadblocks can be destructive of the student's self-concept because they make students defensive, argumentative, resentful, guilty, frustrated, misunderstood, or pressured. Gordon admits, however, that 90% to 95% of teachers in his T.E.T. course respond to students with one of these roadblocks.

The most effective method for preventing communication breakdown is "active listening," procedures which encourage the teacher to move from a more passive role of door openers to a more active role. Active listening involves interaction with the student and feedback from the teacher. Teachers need to develop certain attitudes or "sets" to engage in active listening: trust students' abilities to solve their problems, accept their feelings (while recognizing that they are often transitory), show a desire to help with problems and allocate time for doing so, do not identify too closely with the problems and become upset over them, and respect students' privacy.

T.E.T. tries to answer the question, "Who owns the problem?" When the problem is owned by the student (e.g.: the student cannot find her pencil or the student is daydreaming), then door openers and active listening can be used. If the problem is owned by the teacher (the problem has a concrete effect on the teacher), then "I" messages can be used. Rather than you-messages ("Why did *you* do that?") I-messages ("I can't work because of the messy classroom") put responsibility on the teacher, the person experiencing the problem. By using an I-message, the teacher takes responsibility for listening to her own feelings and communicating them with students. The teacher conveys to students her feelings in a non-blaming, nonjudgmental description. But unless the student believes that the I-message has the claimed effect on the teacher, the message is not likely to have the desired effect. Only when the student believes that his behavior causes the teacher a genuine problem will he be motivated to change. Since most students do not want to be considered "bad guys" and want their teacher to like them, they are therefore likely to modify their behavior.

Gordon presents two types of authority frequently used by teachers. In Method I, the solution acceptable to the teacher is used; whereas in Method II, the solution acceptable to the student is used. In the former method, the teacher wins and the student loses, while in the latter method the teacher loses and the student wins. Young children are dependent on the teacher and therefore the use of rewards and punishment may work with them. Adolescent youth, however, are more independent of the teacher and rewards and punishment are less effective control mechanisms. What students need, according to Gordon, is not the exercise of teacher power and external control but internal control; this comes about when student needs and those with whom they interact are respected.

On the other hand, Method II, a permissive approach, fosters selfishness, unmanageability, loss of respect for the teacher, and chaotic classrooms. Although it may foster more student activity than Method I, the teacher pays a high price for it. It does not foster high morale because students dislike the unruly class conditions and the inability to be productive.

What, then, is the alternative to these two methods? Gordon offers

Method III, a conflict resolution approach based on the scientific method of problem-solving as devised by John Dewey; it consists of the following steps:

1. Defining the problem
2. Generating possible solutions
3. Evaluating the solutions
4. Deciding which solution is best
5. Determining how to implement the decision
6. Assessing how well the solution solved the problem

Although these are not precisely Dewey's steps, this version should prove functional in dealing with conflicts. Method III is a "no-lose" conflict-resolving approach that involves the teacher and students working together cooperatively to reflectively solve conflicts. Gordon believes that when Method III is used no resentment is generated, motivation improves, and creative thinking is promoted. The method does not require persuasion to accept it, teacher power is not required, students become more responsible, and they learn to deal with genuine problems.

Method III, however, will not likely work when there is a value conflict because the student does not see that a problem exists and therefore will not negotiate. Neither of the other two methods is effective in this situation because, with Method I, the teacher's show of power intensifies the student's conviction in his own values and, with Method II, it permits the student to do what he wants but at the expense of the teacher's values. Instead Gordon recommends that the teacher can become a consultant to students on value issues and approach the relationship non-judgmentally. A second technique is to model the desired behavior and to maintain good relations with students so they will want to model the observed behavior. Teachers can also try to change themselves, and they can also learn to be serene when they have failed to overcome a value conflict and to learn to accept what they have been unable to change.

In evaluating Teacher Effectiveness Training, the program may help teachers to communicate more effectively with students, and it shows teachers how to improve student behavior without the imposition of the teacher's power or coercing students through various commonly-used devices. It helps teachers become empathic listeners and be less judgmental and more open to students. T.E.T. also shows teachers how to resolve conflicts by using a problem-solving approach, and it thereby helps students to think reflectively by cooperatively engaging in this process with their teacher. Finally, T.E.T. wisely recognizes that value conflicts are not usually amenable to problem-solving techniques but require other approaches.

Although Gordon presents many examples of communication skills, there is a problem of translating these skills into classroom situations. Practice exercises are needed to help the teacher develop and perfect these skills.

The distinction between "teacher-owned problems" and "student-owned problems" is unclear. In some places, the teacher's honest feelings toward students are what is meant by a teacher-owned problem; whereas in other places, Gordon restricts the meaning to student behavior that has a real, tangible, or concrete effect upon the teacher.

The teacher's conventional procedure is disarmed by repudiating such moves as ordering, advising, lecturing, praising, and the like. While some of these linguistic moves should be avoided — such as threatening, labeling, moralizing, and being sarcastic — it is less clear that advising, giving logical arguments, analyzing, diagnosing, praising, and sympathizing should also be avoided. What Gordon has done is to lump together diverse linguistic moves; of these, a prima facie case can be made against some of them, while with others the evidence against them is far from definitive — in fact, some may be quite valuable and should be retained. For instance, analyzing and diagnosing should be retained and freely employed, while praising should be used circumspectly because it does not always have the desired effect.

The reason why Gordon lumps these linguistic moves together under the heading of "roadblocks" is that he is following Rogers' client-centered therapy by taking a nondirective, nonjudgmental stance. This brings us to the primary weakness of T.E.T.: its grounding in Rogerian psychology.

T.E.T. may actually require some techniques that are better suited to therapy, and since teachers are neither trained as therapists nor authorized to engage in therapy with their classes, they may do more harm than good. The therapeutic origins of T.E.T. should be clearly identified so that teachers can determine in which aspects they are competent and are justified in employing.

In the attempt to be nondirective and nonjudgmental, Gordon does not recognize that the techniques he recommends and the ones eschewed are expressions of his values and judgments. Thus teachers must be judgmental in selecting his system because they are saying something about what they value. The difference with a conventional approach to discipline is not that in one approach the teacher has endorsed a set of values and avoided doing so with T.E.T.; rather, the difference is that in

T.E.T. the teacher tends to model values, while more conventional teachers explicitly prescribe values. It would be better for Gordon to make the values and the ethical basis for his position explicit to the reader and provide some justification for it.

Gordon borrows from Rogers' nondirective approach whereby the teacher remains nonjudgmental with students and open to their various modes of expression. This may help students to gain insight into themselves, but it is less likely to lead to significant behavior change because no set of devices, other than problem-solving, are provided for students to gain a better grip on their behavior. All of the techniques are designed for the teacher; and although by changing the way teachers relate to students may effect some changes in student behavior, more thorough and long-lasting change is likely to occur when combined with techniques for students that are clear, direct, and easily utilized.

THE SOCIAL LITERACY APPROACH

Alfred Altschuler, a professor at the University of Massachusetts at Amherst, developed his social literacy approach as a result of his experiences and observations in the United States and Latin America. He bases his approach on Paulo Freire's educational philosophy, problem-solving processes, and dialog relationships.[9] The Social Literacy Approach is organized into goals and methods. The goals section presents a synopsis of Freire's philosophy and some theoretical and strategic considerations; the methods section attempts to show how to resolve conflicts through dialog, raise consciousness, utilize the problem-posing process, and even handle mainstreaming, minimum competencies, and burnout. Social literacy focuses on prevention whereas most approaches, says Altschuler, are remedial and situation specific.

By posing questions with others, it should be possible to locate the conflict-producing roles and rules. By searching for generative themes (the central conflicts), it should be possible to show how the system victimizes those involved. And through democratic dialog, it should be possible to change the system by overcoming conflict and making it easier for people to love.

The approach was initially employed in 1971 in the Springfield, Massachusetts school where observations were made to identify key variables; then in 1976 funding was obtained from USOE, which was used for training one hundred teachers from ten schools in an intensive three-week workshop; but no follow-up by independent evaluators was reported.

One objective of social literacy is to move participants from either a belief that the situation of oppression is an unchangeable fact of existence or that the problem lies in the individuals who deviate from the rules and roles of the system to the critical-transforming stage where the problem is recognized in the conflict-producing, oppressive roles and rules of the system that victimizes participants.

To help individuals, the following activities are employed: a five-step process to identify central conflicts, consciousness-raising exercises, and instructions for problem solving. In laying a groundwork for identifying central conflicts, Altschuler first reflects on what Freire means by the statement: "To speak a true word is to transform the world." This statement means more than issuing factually accurate statements; it is more of an act of creation. Specifically, true words are spoken or written, they have existential meaning (they relate meaningfully to the hearer or reader's experience), name problems, are heard and get reactions, are embedded in dialog, and are a commitment.

To identify an organization's central conflicts the following steps are used: list the organization's special vocabulary, prioritize the list, determine whether the top word signifies a central conflict (in the sense that many organizational conflicts are found in this issue), be certain that it is a problem or situation open to resolution, and speak true words.

Raising consciousness involves cultivating a greater cognizance of oppression. "Oppression exists," says Altschuler, "whenever there is economic exploitation or whenever an individual's development is blocked."[10] One needs to progress through different stages in order to raise consciousness. In the magical-conforming stage, difficulties are viewed as unchangeable and inevitable facts of existence. The naive-reforming stage views the causes of problems as deviation from the rules and regulations of the system. In the critical-transforming stage, individuals develop skills in identifying the system's roles and rules that oppress. Altschuler uses case studies in which conflicts are presented to help persons raise their consciousness.

The problem-solving process consists of four steps: name the problematic incident; identify patterns of conflict; brainstorm alternate solutions to change the rules and roles that govern people's behavior; and develop democratic plans for implementing a solution.

The social literacy approach differs from any previously considered by seeking the source of oppression and attempting to raise consciousness and engage in problem-solving to transform the system. Other models identify the source of the problem in disruptive students, inadequate ability of teachers to relate effectively to students, or a combination of these. Altschuler has performed a vital service by calling attention to oppressive roles and rules that victimize participants. He has also provided a number of useful techniques for identifying central conflicts, raising consciousness, and solving problems.

But despite the likely merits of the methodology, it does not seem that it could be used successfully just by reading the book; it would probably be necessary to listen to the eight audio-cassette tapes about the program and participate in a social literacy group conducted by an experienced group leader.

Although Altschuler has imaginatively grounded his model in Freire's philosophy of education, the problem may be in uncritically adopting some of Freire's ideas. Freire's aim is to help people become more fully human and to help overcome the conditions of oppression that prevent its realization. The fully human aim, however, seems to commit the naturalistic fallacy (deriving what *ought* to be from what *is* the case). Nevertheless, it is still a seductive aim until one realizes how widely it has been resisted. Those opposing the fully human aim include those holding humans to be innately wicked or brutish (Calvinists and Hobbesians), creators of a higher man (Nietzschians and Shavians), self-transcenders (some idealists), opponents of shaping youth toward a desired end (some romantics), devotees of transcending humankind and emerging with a higher being or consciousness (most mystics), and potential transformers of human nature (eugenicists and genetic engineers).

Freire says that "any situation in which 'A' objectively exploits 'B' or hinders his pursuit of self-affirmation as a responsible person is one of oppression."[11] But he still needs to state criteria for oppression in order that it can be precisely determined and difficult cases be resolved. Altschuler accepts Freire's notion but ties oppression, as noted earlier, to economic exploitation or the blocking of individual development. But dividing the world into oppressors and oppressed, as Altschuler has done by following Freire, greatly oversimplifies because it fails to consider sufficiently the distribution and uses of power, economic realities, and the operations of social-class systems. Thus the social-literacy approach of exclusively blaming the system is an oversimplification and a distortion. More suitable approaches are available to ascribe collective responsibility.[12] But despite the misgivings just cited, it is still a bold and imaginative approach that merits considerable attention and field testing.

GLASSER'S DEFICIENCY MODEL

William Glasser, a Los Angeles psychiatrist, developed reality therapy to deal with behavior problems. Rather than seeking to uncover events in one's past that may have caused one's present problems, he focuses on the present and situations currently confronting the individual. He extended his reality therapy from psychiatry to deal with recalcitrant school disciplinary problems.

Glasser uses a deficiency model to explain these problems. Disciplinary problems, he believes, arise out of need deficiencies and can be overcome by fulfilling certain essential needs. One reason that people do not fulfill their needs, Glasser claims, is that they deny the reality of the world around them; therefore, they must face reality and be shown how to fulfill their needs. Needs are fulfilled by being involved with people — at least one person but preferably more; and these other people must be in touch with reality and able to fulfill their own needs. "Therefore, essential to fulfillment of our needs is a person, preferably a group of people, with whom we are emotionally involved *from the time we are born to the time we die.*"[13]

All people have the same needs, but they vary in their capacity to fulfill them. Reality therapy focuses on helping patients fulfill their need to be loved (from friendship to conjugal love) and the need to feel worthwhile to others and to self. The two needs are interrelated insofar as one who is loved will usually feel worthwhile. Even though there may be persons in our lives who claim to care for us, one may not care for them or be able to accept their love.

Responsibility is a key to understanding reality therapy. Glasser presents a stipulated definition of responsibility as "the ability to fulfill one's needs, and to do so in a way that does not deprive others of the ability to fulfill their needs."[14] In light of this definition, the responsible person has good mental health and the irresponsible person is mentally ill. (Glasser prefers to do away with psychiatric terms associated with the mentally ill.)

Glasser insists that the teacher should try to change behavior rather than attitudes; for if we wait for attitudinal change, it stalls behavior improvement, but not the converse. The student must succeed in one important aspect of life in order to succeed in general.

It is possible, irrespective of the child's background, to succeed in school — and school success, he claims, gives one an excellent chance for success in life. But deficiency needs of love and self-worth preclude success. These needs are related to the concept of identity, which enables each individual to feel of some importance. One gains an identity through the home and school, and the acquisition of a successful identity motivates the student toward goals. Parents should help their children but let them take responsiblity for finding personal goals; this can be facilitated by relating the good feelings about oneself to reasonable goals.[15]

In handling disciplinary problems the teacher should help the student plan a better course of behavior, and once a student makes a commitment to change, then no excuse is accepted for failing to do so. Punishment, Glasser contends, is usually arbitrary and does not work. Discipline, in contrast, asks the student to evaluate and take responsibility for behavior.

The teacher should make learning experiences relevant by relating subjects to the lives of students and avoid conveying the idea that there is one right answer and that everything worthwhile can be measured and assigned a value. Glasser is opposed to tracking, grades, sarcasm and ridicule.

Students should have a voice in developing and applying classroom rules; there should be reasonable rules that are firmly enforced and supported by brief periodic classroom meetings to discuss discipline problems. Although he favors abolishing rules whenever students show sufficient maturity to do without them, he believes that a permissive classroom is destructive for unsuccessful students because it generates student antagonism and a feeling that the teacher does not care about them.

The teacher, Glasser believes, should relate personally to the student and set firm disciplinary limits. Minor disciplinary problems can be handled in home-room meetings; special groups, however, are necessary to handle major problems. Few meetings should be held with parents about discipline because parents usually get upset and punish the child. Whenever such meetings are held, they should be restricted to finding ways to solve the problem rather than finding fault. "Teachers have the responsibility for making education relevant and interesting; students have the responsiblity *to attend class, to study, and to learn.*"[16]

Glasser uses the following eight steps to get disruptive students to assume responsibility for their behavior.

1. The student is confronted and told to stop the undesirable behavior. This means that the teacher uses directive statements ("Get back to your seat."), but does not berate or insult the student. The teacher follows with a statement of correct behavior ("Stay in your seat until you complete the assignments.").

2. Ask "What" questions.
   The objective of using questions is to get the students to think about his or her actions; the point is not to evoke excuses but to elicit a statement from the student about the behavior. Excuses are not accepted; rather, the student is asked to consider the consequences of the action.
3. Develop a plan or commitment.
   The student is asked to develop a plan or commitment to rectify the misbehavior. It is important that it be a plan worked out with the student, not a teacher imposed plan. The teacher must never accept excuses for failing to live up to the plan. Glasser asks the student to sign a written pledge to honor the plan.
4. Logical consequences.
   The student must follow the consequences of adhering to or violating the plan. When the student follows the plan successfully, certain privileges are awarded; and when the plan is violated, certain privileges are withdrawn. The student must perceive these activities as privileges before they will be successful. For instance, helping the teacher decorate the bulletin boards may be seen as a privilege for some students but not for others.
5. Class isolation.
   Persistent failure to carry out the plan leads to the teacher's next step: class isolation of the student. The student is given a place to listen and observe in the classroom but isolated from the other students so that the offending student can have time to think seriously about fulfilling the plan.
6. In-school isolation.
   Whenever the student disturbs others from the isolation area or refuses to carry out the plan when returned to regular classroom activities, the teacher proceeds to in-school isolation. An in-school suspension area in the principal's office, a storage room, or a room set aside for this purpose is used. Here the student is expected to remain, under the supervision of the principal or guidance counselor, until the student has devised an acceptable plan and shown an earnestness to follow it by displaying acceptable classroom behavior. Parents are not involved in the problem at this stage. The principal repeats steps 1 through 5.
7. Outside-of-school isolation.
   If a student cannot develop a plan and exhibit minimal self-control, then the parents are contacted and the student is temporarily suspended from school in the parents' care. Upon the student's return to school, the principal and teacher repeat steps 1 through 6.

8. Referred to an outside agency.
   When the previous steps fail and the student has to repeatedly be sent home, the student is referred to a special school or an outside community agency.

Glasser's model has a number of significant strengths and weaknesses that should be carefully considered before implementation. Glasser offers a structured program that could readily be put into practice; it is clearly stated and reasonably well organized. Another strong feature is that it shows how to cultivate discipline without resorting to punishment. Glasser also recommends that the teacher should relate personally with the student and teach relevant material. His program achieves a balance for learning failures (as contrasted to Kohl's and Altschuler's models) by having teachers and students share distinctive responsibilities.

Glasser's model, however, is afflicted with several problems. He talks about people denying reality and therefore having to be taught how to face it. But this way of talking glosses over certain substantive metaphysical questions that philosophers have struggled with for generations. What he probably means is that when an individual is acting responsibly, then that person is surely in touch with reality. This way of phrasing it, however, tells us more about psychological adjustment than resolving any questions about what is reality.

In contrast to Freud, Glasser wants to judge maladjustment and school failures in moral terms. This raises some questions over which there currently is a division of opinion. Is it ethically right to do so? And if right, what are the moral principles involved? And even if it is ethical, is it pedagogically and therapeutically sound? Since Glasser deviates here from established practice, he should offer a more complete and adequate justification.

Central to Glasser's system is the needs-deficiency model. These needs are deficiency or basic needs rather than derived needs (activities or processes used to satisfy basic needs such as learning to handle money or how to cook). In making statements about what an individual needs, the need actually exists to fulfill some objective ("he needs to learn to read in order to hold a job"). In such cases a need is recognized as such only if it fulfills a desired objective. Whether an objective is desirable is determined by a set of values or a philosophy of education. Glasser, unfortunately, has focused primarily on the needs and not the objectives and has spoken of objectives often in negative terms of eliminating school failure rather than a set of positive outcomes supported by a justifiable set of values.

Glasser fails to demonstrate that the two needs he cites are actually deficiency needs and that their fulfillment will overcome psychiatric problems and school failures. Psychologists who use a needs approach often disagree on basic needs. For instance, Abraham Maslow has postulated a hierarchy of needs that largely differs from Glasser's approach.[17] Some psychotherapists would also disagree that a deficiency in love or affection from another significant person or group will inevitably lead to emotional illness or, in Glasser's term, "irresponsibility."[18] Empirical evidence is mixed. Some research studies do not support the use in classrooms of reality-therapy methods for improving self-concept, whereas other studies do provide some support.[19]

DREIKURS' LOGICAL CONSEQUENCES

Rudolf Dreikurs (1897-1972) was a professor of psychiatry at Chicago Medical School and later director of the Alfred Adler Institute in Chicago. Influenced by Adler, he specialized in family-child counseling and classroom behavior.

Dreikurs holds that basic to all human beings is the desire to be part of the group. The child is born with an innate potential to function as a social being and to develop social feeling, which leads to cooperation and fulfillment, while any restriction in its development leads to limited ability to function as a social being.[20]

Behavior, according to Dreikurs, is purposive or goal-directed. It is only when the goal is identified and understood that behavior makes sense. The individual is not a puppet of her past but can exercise self-determination. Nevertheless, the child does not understand why she does something wrong or misbehaves; the educator must help the child understand herself and her goals.[21]

A well-behaved and well-adjusted child conforms to the group by making useful contributions. But even those who misbehave believe that their actions will give them social status. Four goals of disturbing behavior can be found with young children up to the age of ten; they can also be found in teenagers and adults but are not inclusive, as adolescents can use such other measures as sex, smoking, heroism, and excitement. These goals are: attention-getting, power, revenge, and inadequacy.[22]

Our culture provides few oportunities for children to establish their social position through useful contributions and therefore the attention getting mechanism (AGM) arises in most children. Since most of what is done in the family is handled by parents or older siblings, children have little chance to gain status constructively. The child may seek attention through charm and affection; but since doing so does not enhance self-reliance, the child will constantly seek new proof of worthiness even if it results in punishment or humiliation so long as he achieves his purpose. In school, the child seeks to be recognized in class and feel a sense of belonging. Rather than gain recognition through productive classwork, the child may use AGM as a means of acceptance. The child may ask the teacher for special favors, constant help on assignments, refuse to work without teacher attention, ask irrelevant questions, and the like.

Power seeking goes beyond the attention getting mechanism. The child who feels inferior and incapable of measuring up to expectations will seek power irrespective of whether she is actually handicapped or only perceives herself as inadequate. Efforts by the teacher to control the child lead to a struggle for power and superiority, with the child attempting to prove she can do what she wants and refuse to do what the teacher says she ought to do. The child will win this struggle in most cases because her fighting methods are not restricted by moral obligations or responsibility. The child seeks to defeat those who suppress her and gain status among her peers by thwarting the teacher's will. Once a power struggle between teacher and student ensues, their relationship will deteriorate and likely move to the next goal: seeking revenge.

Children who believe that others are unfair to them, hurt them, and disregard their feelings seek revenge. They no longer seek attention or power because the mutual antagonism with the teacher is sufficient for the desire of retaliation to emerge. Feeling ostracized and disliked, they believe they can only regain their place in the group by making themselves hated. They regard themselves triumphant when they are vicious because this is the only triumph they can attain. But these children seek revenge against anyone, not just those that they believe have hurt them; therefore, they are likely to hit other children, scribble on their papers, kick, or scratch them, insult others and use obscenities. Since they are convinced that nobody likes them and their goal is always to be right, they strike out at others and use it as proof that they are disliked.

Some children at an early age believe that there is no chance to find a place for themselves and therefore they move toward a display of inadequacy. Other children, after unsuccessful attempts to find significance through attention getting, power, or revenge become discouraged and move toward the goal of inadequacy. They expect only defeat and failure, become passive and stop trying. By failing to participate, they try to avoid more embarrassing and humiliating experiences.

How does the teacher recognize the child's goals? When the teacher feels annoyed at a child who does not respond to reminding or coaxing, the child usually wants attention. The teacher who feels challenged or threatened is likely faced with power-seeking behavior. Whereas the teacher who feels hurt is facing a child who wants revenge. And finally, the teacher who feels helpless and defeated is dealing with a child who exhibits inadequacy.

Another way to determine the child's goal is to observe how the child responds to the teacher's reprimand. The child who stops her behavior and then starts again is seeking attention. The child is usually seeking power when he continues his behavior and even intensifies despite the reprimand. If a child becomes angry and abusive, she is likely seeking revenge. And the child feels inadequacy if she does nothing after being reprimanded.

Teachers need to confront children with their misbehavior in a nonthreatening way to expose their faulty goals. The teacher asks the child whether she knows why she acted a certain way. Although the child does not know, the question is necessary before moving to the next step of telling the child what the teacher believes the goal to be. The goal is presented as a guess in the form of "could it be that _____?"
(Attention) Could it be that you want me to notice you more?
(Power) Could it be that you want to be boss?
(Revenge) Could it be that you want to get even?
(Inadequacy) Could it be that you want to be left alone because you are afraid to fail?

A number of tactics can be used in correcting the different forms of undesirable behavior. In handling attention getting behavior, the teacher should discuss the goal with the child. The teacher should develop a plan with the child that takes into consideration how often the child wants to be recognized during the day.

After discussing the goal with the child who seeks power, the teacher should avoid getting into a power struggle, watch for opportunities for cooperation, express pleasure at the child's progress, and do the unexpected by not reacting overtly to the child's provocation.

The revengeful child needs to be confronted with his goal. The teacher should discuss with the child situations where he provoked others, but point out to him his good qualities that he fails to use to make himself more likeable. The child is asked to try a plan whereby he does not provoke anyone for a certain length of time to see if others like him. The teacher avoids retaliation, expresses empathy, and engages the child in group discussion and promotes group acceptance.

The child with inadequate behavior is shown her goals and told that her true ability cannot be demonstrated without trying. The child should be assured that when she tries to do the work and is unable to do so, the teacher and students will help her; however, it is important to give the child the type of work with which she is likely to succeed. The teacher should enlist group discussion and group assistance to help overcome the behavior.

Children will misbehave if they see they have no opportunity to succeed and face only discouraging experiences. Neither indulgence and overprotection on the one hand nor humiliation and punishment on the other will rectify behavior because both approaches deprive children of learning to take care of themselves and to overcome problems. Children need self-confidence and courage for social adjustment and academic progress. Teachers, however, are faced with children who are already handicapped by undesirable home training and expect to be treated similarly in school. Early experiences in school are critical and, when not handled properly, adults can be left with a strong distaste for formal knowledge or become convinced that they are incapable of spelling or computing correctly.

The child seldom changes undesirable behavior patterns when criticized; instead, it is important for teachers to offer encouragement. But the use of encouragement, according to Dreikurs, requires careful observation and practice because what is encouraging to one child may not be to another: the teacher may expect too little or too much of a child and having erroneous expectations will lead to the child's discouragement. How these expectations are defined are based on the child's perception. Encouragement, to be effective, depends more upon attitudes than specific acts; it depends less on what is said and done than how one goes about doing it.

But is encouragement just a fancy name for "praise"? Dreikurs believes that praise must be used cautiously because if overdone the child will become dependent upon adult expectations and frightened that she may be unable to measure up to these expectations. It is much more important that the child realize that she has permanent value, that this value is not dissipated by temporary failures and shortcomings. Our present system of classroom competition, however, makes it difficult for the child to maintain this conviction and feel socially secure. A competitive atmosphere erodes fruitful group relations and discourages team work and the sharing of ideas. Each child can make her own contribution without her work being compared to others.

Some parents, however, want schools to foster competition as preparation for a highly competitive society. Dreikurs contends that this is a fallacious assumption because the less competitive a person, the better he can stand up under extreme competition. Those content to do their job are not disturbed by what their competitor may do or achieve; whereas a competitive person can handle competition only when he is succeeding.

Returning to the difference between praise and encouragement, praise puts the emphasis on the child; encouragement places it on the task. Specifically, praise is generally given when a task is well done or completed successfully; encouragement is needed during the task when effort is expended and when a child fails. Praise may stimulate rivalry, while encouragement will more likely foster cooperation. With praise, the child feels judged; with encouragement, the person feels accepted.

Dreikurs also opposes punishment and substitutes natural and logical consequences. Punishment, he says, is an outdated and ineffective disciplinary measure because children retaliate as a consequence of their inability to perceive a relationship between the punishment and the offense.

As a substitute, natural consequences is one measure used. These consequences are not arranged but simply occur. A child plays with a knife and cuts himself or plays with a hot iron and burns himself. The child discovers for himself and learns self-discipline and internal motivation.

Dreikurs distinguishes between applied logical consequences and logical consequences. The former are applied when a child misbehaves but the consequences have not been discussed with the class. Applied logical consequences are a one-time procedure and relate directly to the behavior. The child spills paint on the floor and is given responsibility for getting it up.

Logical consequences are discussed, understood, and accepted by the child. This approach can be used only where a good relationship is established between the teacher and the child; otherwise the child may consider the treatment as a form of punishment. A logical consequence would be that children who damage school property will have to replace it. Logical consequences must be applied consistently and, where possible, children are to be given a choice. For instance, where the child in line is pushing, the child is given a choice either to stop pushing or be taken out of the line and held by the hand. Logical consequences, however, work best in correcting attention getting behavior; this procedure should not be used when safety may be jeopardized, nor when power, revenge, or indifference are the goals. When these are the goals, the child is too busy asserting his superiority or trying to get even that he does not care about the consequences of his acts.

The Dreikurs model has many strong points. It is, above all, a goal-directed purposive model. The significance of recognizing goal-directed behavior is to assume that individuals have some free will, that they can choose and make decisions for themselves and build their own future. This is opposed to a model that claims that individuals are nothing more than the sum total of environmental stimuli that condition them from birth, or that they are the mere instruments of biological drives.

This model is probably the strongest and most firmly grounded psychological approach studied so far. It explains social needs and the need for group belonging; it also explains disruptive behavior without oversimplification by reducing everything to a single cause. Thus disruptive behavior varies with the individual and may stem from any one of four behavioral syndromes. It also shows that, with the teacher's help, students can assume responsibility for correcting their behavior. Dreikurs' theory, in following Adler, does not assume, as Freud has done, that the causes of behavior lie deep in the unconscious and can only be uncovered after years of intensive psychoanalysis. Instead, Dreikurs shows that the causes of problem behavior, while not necessarily superficial or self-evident, can be uncovered by teachers when properly trained.

Dreikurs provides a number of different ways of identifying and treating problem behavior. He shows how to recognize the child's goals by, first of all, identifying how the teacher feels about the child's behavior; second, by determining how the child responds to the teacher's reprimand; and third, by showing how to answer lead questions that will uncover the goal. Dreikurs then gives the teacher specfic tactics for transforming the four types of problem behavior.

The distinctions between encouragement and reward, and between natural and logical consequences, are important contributions (assuming these distinctions can be made in practice). The dangers of punishment, especially the kind where teachers become angry and lose their patience and objectivity with students, are commonly recognized. Less recognized, however, are the dangers of a system of rewards; consequently, encouragement is substituted so that the emphasis is placed on the task rather than the child and allegedly prevents the child from becoming overly dependent upon adult reinforcement for motivation rather than becoming self-directed.

Dreikurs' strictures against competition are based on psychological evidence that shows competition erodes security and healthy group relations.

Most importantly, he contends that the less competitive person can handle extreme competition better because his focus, in contrast to the competitive person, is on the task itself rather than success or failure.

Despite the numerous strong points cited above, Dreikurs' system exhibits certain problems. He holds that it is basic to humans to want to be part of the group, and he speaks of the well behaved and well adjusted child who conforms to the group by making useful contributions. Even those who misbehave, he claims, believe that their action will give them social status. Thus Dreikurs' world is one where all action, whether desirable or undesirable behavior, is an attempt to gain group status; it is a conforming world where the norms of the group are given, not questioned. But these norms should be questioned because it would be unacceptable to conform to an undesirable system or immoral demands. Moreover, if schools seek to develop independent persons, they should teach students to question, gather reliable evidence, and reflectively determine acceptable courses of action rather than feel compelled to conform to the group. At times it will be desirable to conform to the group and at other times refuse to conform; however, the grounds for making these decisions need to be independently determined in each case.

Dreikurs admits that his explanation of problem behavior is insufficient for adolescent behavior, as adolescents use such other measures as "sex, smoking, heroism, and excitement" and are therefore not limited to the four goals of children (up to the age of ten). But, then, how should school discipline problems in the secondary school be handled? What features of Dreikurs' system can be applied there? Since it is insufficient, what supplements are needed for adolescents? These questions remain unanswered. Perhaps it would be best for secondary teachers to adopt one of the previously discussed models or supplement Dreyfus' system with one of them.

Criticisms of the use of reward and punishment are well taken, but Dreikurs' substitution of encouragement and natural and logical consequences are probably conceptually meaningful but problematic in practice. Dreyfus admitted as much by admonishing teachers to guard against permitting logical consequences to degenerate into forms of punishment. "The teacher," Dreyfus says, "needs to help the children to understand the subtle differences between logical consequences and traditional forms of punishment. . . There is no pat formula for applying logical consequences. . . *When* to do *what* and to *whom* requires judgment about many imponderables because every situation is unique."[23] Thus there may be a conceptual basis for encouragement and natural and logical consequences but a problem in classroom application. Despite these criticisms, the Dreikurs model offers a significant contribution in explaining and coping with children's disciplinary problems.

BEHAVIOR MODIFICATION

Behavior modification is based on the psychology of behaviorism founded by John B. Watson. In his system he sought to make psychology a full-fledged science.[24] Watson's behaviorism is based on a stimulus-response model: given the stimulus, psychology could predict the response; and, on the other hand, if given the response, the nature of the effective stimulus could be specified.[25]

Behaviorism, as he saw it, should become empirical in approach and discard all references to consciousness and mental states. Instead, the study of the human organism was to concentrate on overt and observable forms of behavior generated from the muscles, tissues, and glands. Watson was reductionistic in his claim that all behavior can be interpreted in physical-chemical terms. The workings of the nervous system and glands could be observed in their manifestations in overt behavior. Human behavior, he held, can actually be reduced to a sensory-central-motor reaction. It involves a chain of incoming stimuli along the sensory nerves to the central nervous system and then outward over neural pathways to the muscular system for overt response. Memory, too, was explained reductionistically as created by residues of sensory stimulation combined with kinesthetic elements of the mouth muscles in implicit speech processes.

Watson was an environmentalist in the nature-nurture controversy. Humans, he held, have only the instincts of fear, rage, and love, and these were limited in comparison with the importance of experience. He declared that if he were given a dozen healthy infants he could take one at random and make of him any type of specialist — doctor, lawyer, thief, etc.[26] This development would take place through education, which for Watson is nothing more than conditioning. The emotions as well, derived as they are from the basic instincts of fear, rage, and love, are developed by means of conditioning. Personality, in this scheme of things, is considered the end-product of habit systems.

B. F. Skinner, the most influential contemporary behaviorist, differs with Watson in limiting the function of his system to description rather than the customary goal of explanation. His position attempts to avoid Watson's reductionism by defining concepts in terms of observables rather than reducing them to physiological states. Private events, such as a toothache, can be treated as an inference rather than an observable fact.[27] The task of psychology is to find out what the relationship is between the stimulus controlled by the researcher, the other experimental variables, and the response of the subject.

There are two types of behavior: respondent and operant. Behavior is called "respondent," when it is correlated to "specific eliciting stimuli" (as when the dog learns to salivate at the sound of the bell); behavior is "operant" when no stimuli are present. "Stimulus" means any modification of the environment, and a "response" is a part of the behavior. A "reflex" is any observed correlation between stimulus and response."

Conditioning in the form of respondent behavior was used by Skinner in his experiments with pigeons. Reinforcement (reward) was dependent upon the response. Whenever the pigeon exhibited the desired behavior as a result of the stimuli, the response was reinforced by providing food. On the other hand, with operant conditioning the response comes first and then it becomes reinforced. It is through operant conditioning that the efficiency of behavior is improved. This form of conditioning builds a repertoire by which we handle such processes as walking, playing games, using tools, and other activities.

Behavior modification has been shaped by behaviorism by focusing on overt behavior and conditioning. It is based largely on *positive reinforcement* (rewards) rather than *negative reinforcement* (punishment or depriving students of something they want). Behavior modification, therefore, seeks to reinforce desired behavior and promote learning by providing positive support in small steps that reinforce all forms of desirable behavior and achievement. Although Skinner opposed punishment and opted for positive reinforcement, behavior modification advocates punishing students for misbehavior if positive reinforcement would be too slow and ineffective; however, punishment is eschewed and punishment can be imposed only after informing students what is expected of them.

Behavior modification has been applied to a wide range of behavior: oral language and speech,[29] social-emotional behavior,[30] self-control,[31] thoughts and feelings about oneself,[32] and other problem areas. These different applications of behavior modification share certain basic assumptions. The focus is, first of all, on behavior rather than some underlying states. Second, all behavioral change is produced by altering the individual's environment. Finally, treatment is best conducted by direct observation and recording of problem behavior before, during, and after treatment. The number of principles used to explain behavior is small, but the number of different forms of treatment is large.

Since positive reinforcement is central to behavior modification, a closer look at it is in order. Three types of positive reinforcement[33] can be identified: first, token reinforcement that offers students a tangible item after exhibiting desirable behavior (e.g., a ticket to a basketball game, a transistor radio); second, social reinforcement that takes the form of teacher attention, praise and approval; third, primary reinforcement that provides any tangible item that satisfies a biological need (e.g., popcorn, fruit juice, cereal).

Social reinforcement is less obvious than the other two types. The teacher can manifest positive reinforcement by showing approval for desirable behavior in the form of personal attention, praise, smiles, nods, an O.K. sign, a pat on the back. Rather than punish undesirable behavior, the teacher can seek to extinguish it by removing any reinforcement; this is accomplished by ignoring such behavior.

Modeling is another technique used in behavior modification. Individuals are capable of learning from observing the behavior of others. The basic paradigm for this type of learning is to observe a model and then be expected to perform the same behavior as the model. Modeling can be conducted with live models, the use of films and videotapes. Students may choose models from their peers, adults or fictitious characters. The teacher as well, whether consciously or not, is modeling behavior. For instance, the teacher who wants students to exercise self-control should not become angry, shrill, or physically aggressive with students. And the teacher who expects students to be orderly and neat should also manifest these characteristics in both dress and care of the classroom.

Another approach to minimize deviant behavior is to teach poor delinquent youths competitive skills that will provide them with rewards; and to teach interpersonal skills to minimize antisocial behavior of middle class youth. By programming these desirable behaviors properly, they will be strengthened and the deviant behaviors will diminish.[34]

Behavior modification offers a number of advantages. It is a systematic approach that can be learned effectively by teachers in a reasonably short time. The principles can be incorporated into the teaching act and become natural aspects of teaching behavior. Desirable results can be achieved in a relatively short time. At first the teacher may have to spend some time in getting a schedule of reinforcement established, but once in place the time spent on reinforcement is not great. Although behavior modification can be used with all students, it has proven especially effective in working with handicapped students. Some undesirable behaviors, such as phobias and obsessions, that have not yielded to other forms of treatment or therapy, have been corrected by behavior modification.

Yet behavior modification is vulnerable in its theory, assumptions, and methodology. As for theory, both Watson's and Skinner's position have salient weaknesses, especially Watson's. By Watson's reduction of thinking, feeling, and perceiving to certain implicit physiological states is a gross oversimplification of these complex processes. The individual becomes nothing more than a stimulus-response organism built primarily by a process of conditioning. Behaviorism as a theory of behavior becomes highly mechanistic, failing to account for purposive behavior and unable to provide a satisfactory explanation for the higher processes of learning in the form of cognitive and affective processes. With the stimulus-response model, based as it is on mechanistic cause and effect assumptions, all novel behavior is impossible; present behavior is primarily conceived as the recapitulation of past behavior established by conditioning.

In contrast, Skinner's method is based on a consistent and persistent inductive empiricism applied rigorously in observation and experimentation, and his approach marks a considerable advance over Watson in sophistication, rigor, and the avoidance of reductionism.

Yet, one may still charge Skinner with adopting scientific methods of the past, for if we wish to be as scientific as possible—as Skinner surely does—one could not imagine the great progress made in the physical sciences during this century if scientists had been content to limit their methodology to description and observation.

Skinner is unable to deal with problems of motivation because of the unobservables and mentalistic concepts that may be needed in such a treatment. The range of experimentation on drives and emotions is restricted by the nature of psychological laboratory procedures. Rather than neglect these areas, it would seem better to change the procedures and framework of inquiry. Furthermore, work in psychotherapy indicates that some type of theoretical explanation of inner behavior is needed in order to successfully treat patients. Our understanding of persons is severely limited when interior life is avoided, when the organism is broken into bits and pieces for their amenability to certain forms of investigation, leaving human purposes, values, and ideals with no place in the study of human behavior.

As for behavior modification, some procedures are only effective with certain age groups. For instance, if the teacher draws up a set of classroom rules and praises students as often as possible whenever they comply with the rules, this type of reinforcement may be effective at the elementary, but not the secondary, level. Secondary students may speak derisively of peers who receive frequent teacher praise, calling them "teacher's pet" and other epithets.

Another problem is that what is taken to be a positive reward varies from student to student. Not all students will value what the teacher anticipates that they will find of worth; not all children like television, rock music, candy, and going to the playground. Moreover, in terms of negative reinforcers, not all students object to staying after school, doing extra homework, or staying in the classroom while others are on the playground.

More seriously, some criticisms can be made of behavior modification not just in terms of its effectiveness in certain situations or with certain age groups but its overall value as a means of discipline. Behavior modification could be charged with dehumanizing learners by treating them as stimulus-response mechanisms that are to be manipulated by respondent and operant conditioning. Learners have no free will; they are merely objects of reinforcement schedules so that classroom order can be maintained. Learners have no interior life, will, motivation, or intention; they are merely organisms that can be subjected to conditioning to comply with the dictates of those in authority. Learners do not exhibit higher cognitive processes and creativity; they are little more than organisms who can be subjected to control by clever schedules of reinforcement. Thus it is questionable whether behavior modification should ever be used exclusively as a means of control.

CANTER'S ASSERTIVE DISCIPLINE

Lee and Marlene Canter have conducted research into teachers who effectively handle discipline in their classrooms and, after testing their system, devised a model of assertive discipline.[35] During the 1970s, an area known as Assertiveness Training emerged in popular psychology that attracted considerable attention among the public.[36] Assertiveness Training held that what you do in relation to others affects your self esteem, and that one can be taught the skills necessary to defend one's basic rights.

Assertive behavior is typically contrasted with nonassertive behavior and aggressive behavior. Nonassertive behavior is characterized by timidity and an inability to communicate directly and openly. This is manifested in fear to make eye contact, inability to engage in small talk, and fear of social situations out of fear of rejection or making mistakes.

Aggressive behavior, on the other hand, is self-enhancing at the expense of others. The aggressive person may make choices for others, depreciate them, gain one's objective by hurting others. Although the aggressive person, in contrast to the non-assertive person, may achieve immediate goals, the actions taken may cause frustration and hatred in others, which may lead to revenge.

In contrast, assertive behavior is self-enhancing, it expresses one's feelings, causes the person to feel good about oneself, and it may achieve the desired goal but in the process is not supposed to hurt others. Thus assertive behavior is expected to permit people to reveal themselves (what they think and feel), communicate with people at different levels (friends, family, strangers), involves taking direct action, and enables a person to maintain self-respect.

As an illustration of these forms of behavior, Jean is invited to a party at a friend's house and Jean, who does not drink, is offered a drink. The nonassertive response would be to accept the drink and pretend that she has no objection to drinking. Although she may be filled with dread and trepidation, she is more worried about what others may think about her, which causes her not to speak up. Whereas if she exhibits aggressive behavior, she becomes exasperated and condemns the person loudly who offered her a drink and demands to be taken home right away to get away from such "disgusting" behavior. In contrast, with assertive behavior, she would quietly decline the drink and tell the person that she does not drink but recognizes the right of others to drink if they so choose.

Assertive discipline is designed to help teachers express their wants and feelings, to stand up for what they desire while not abusing the rights of others; it is an attempt to increase the teacher's ability to meet personal and professional needs. The model emphasizes the teacher gaining full control of the classroom by developing strong assertive skills to establish and maintain order.

This model holds that much of teacher failure is a failure to maintain effective classroom discipline. The teacher should not erroneously shrink from gaining firm control in the classroom, as such control is not stifling but liberating and humane. Assertive discipline maintains a humane atmosphere by recognizing both teacher and student rights.

Assertiveness takes the form of teachers saying "no" without feeling guilty, defending oneself when criticized, giving and receiving compliments gracefully, communicating clearly to students positive expectations, and stating consequences that will occur from student behavior.

The teacher's manner should be composed, firm, consistent, and positive.

Five steps can be used to implement assertive discipline. The first step is to eliminate obstacles to assertive behavior. This means that teachers should rid themselves of negative expectations about students and supplant them with positive ones. Whatever problems students may have, they should not be permitted to engage in destructive behavior or violate the rights of others. Moreover, teachers have the power to influence students positively despite student problems. They also have the right to expect support from principals, other school personnel, and parents.

The second step is to practice the use of assertive behavior. This means that teachers need to eliminate nonassertive and hostile behavior (Canter and Canter use the term "hostile" rather than "aggressive"). Teachers should continue to practice the assertive style until it becomes a natural part of their behavior. The assertive response indicates the teacher's disapproval in a firm, unemotional, businesslike way and informs the students what they are expected to do; it does not condemn, scold, threaten, or blame; neither does it overlook misbehavior or plead with students to act properly. The teacher may have to use the "broken-record" response when students fail to comply by reitering the statement until the students take cognizance of it and correct their behavior. The teacher would firmly reiterate, without raising one's voice, until the desired behavior is attained; however if the desired behavior does not occur after three times, then the teacher should take other action.

The next step is to learn to set limits. Teachers need to analyze the various activities students will be involved in during the school day and the types of behavior expected in these activities. Elementary teachers can post signs about expected behavior at the front of the room; whereas secondary teachers would not use signs but would state desired behaviors. Some techniques advocated (borrowed from Teacher Effectiveness Training) are to give hints or reminders of what is expected, use I-messages, questions, and demands (the latter, however, should only be used as a last resort and only when the teacher is willing to follow through with the consequences).

The fourth step entails following through on limits previously set. The teacher makes promises about action to be taken, not threats. The consequences for misbehavior are established in advance, whether the consequences are loss of privileges, detention, referral to the principal, or soliciting the parents' enforcement of consequences in the home. The consequences should be acceptable to the teacher, disagreeable but not harmful to the student, and should be applied immediately after the undesirable behavior.

The final step is to implement a system of positive assertions. This means to give attention to students who exhibit appropriate behavior and use praise and reward, thereby showing disrupting students that if they are seeking attention, they can more likely receive it by conducting themselves more appropriately. Assertive discipline utilizes a system of positive reinforcement in the form of special awards (positive comments, certificates of accomplishment), material rewards, group rewards (drop marbles into a jar when a group works diligently on a project), favorable notes to parents, and encouraging parents to extend privileges at home.

In evaluating assertive discipline, it should be noted that it places the teacher in command and control of the class without becoming autocratic, as the teacher respects the students' rights and establishes reasonable, not harsh, rules. Assertive discipline shows teachers the weaknesses of being nonassertive or hostile and how to overcome these behavior patterns and adopt a more constructive style.

Assertive discipline also draws upon Teacher Effectiveness Training and behavior modification by seeking to integrate selected appropriate techniques into the assertive discipline framework. Undoubtedly these additional techniques augment and complement assertive behavior.

On the negative side, this is an eclectic model and eclecticism sometimes leads to a hodgepodge of ideas and various inconsistencies. In this case, however, the charge is not sustained because the borrowed material is reasonably well integrated into the system. But a related criticism of electicism — unoriginality — is closer to the mark. The assertive discipline model not only borrows from T.E.T. and behavior modification, but assertiveness training as well. The main task for the Canters was then to develop the role and application of assertive discipline in classroom situations. Since assertive discipline draws from other models, it may be subject to similar criticisms made of those models, especially behavior modification, whenever the other models are used extensively.

Obviously it is better for a teacher to be assertive than to be nonassertive, aggressive, or autocratic; it is less evident, however, that assertiveness itself exhausts all of the desirable behavioral styles. Both Kohl's natural development model and T.E.T. offer a nondirective approach with different objectives that may achieve desirable results and develop a healthy classroom environment. In other words, assertive behavior, a directive approach, is one teacher style that is helpful in maintaining classroom control; other teachers, because of differences in temperament and/or objectives, may cultivate a different style effectively, one that may be less directive and more student-centered.

Discipline problems may be caused by genuine concerns and needs that remain unfulfilled. Assertive discipline, though it recognizes that students have basic rights that should be acknowledged, does not try to understand and treat these deeper concerns and needs; in this sense it is similar to behavior modification and dissimilar to Dreikurs' model. There is some question whether teachers are actually prepared to deal with these deeper problems or should refer the student to a specialist. Nevertheless, in contrast to the models of Dreikurs and Glasser, assertive discipline offers scant psychological explanations of disruptive behavior.

COMPARISON OF MODELS

Theory

In this section a selective comparison will be made of the different models in the chapter in terms of their theory; in the next section, methodology and application will be explored. Such comparisons should help to crystalize one's views, provide needed connections, and help the reader reach firmer conclusions.

The three models that are undergirded by the most developed psychological theory are Glasser's Deficiency Model, Dreikurs' Logical Consequences, and Behavior Modification. Of the three, the theory of behavior modification appears to be more distorted because it reduces humans to reactive organisms with no interior life and no way to account for higher cognitive processes and creativity. In contrast, both Dreikurs and Glasser recognize a complexity of human needs and desires that cannot be reduced to simple stimulus-response bonds. But Glasser talks about basic unfulfilled human needs that may cause students to be disruptive, yet it is not clear that his methodology actually fulfills those needs; rather, he shows teachers how to get students to assume outward responsibility for their acts. Dreikurs, however, shapes his model on the observation that children's problem behavior takes the form of attention getting, power, revenge, or inadequacy. In other words, Dreikurs probably has the soundest psychological explanation for problem behavior.

The only model that rests on a philosophy is the Social Literacy Approach, which is based on Paul Freire's revolutionary philosophy. What this does is to provide the model with a more substantial justification for its knowledge and value claims than any of the other models. But one should not confuse a substantial and well developed justification with an acceptable one, as some teachers will reject the philosophy because it is too radical or for some other reason.

T.E.T. draws upon Carl Rogers' nondirective counseling theory. The question here is not the adequacy of Rogers' theory for counseling but its adequacy for classroom settings. Although teachers are shown how to adopt a nondirective, nonjudgmental stance, T.E.T. may actually require some techniques more suitable for therapy.

While Kohl draws upon progressivist theory and more recent work in the open classroom movement, he would have had a firmer foundation if he had also employed some of Dewey's philosophy. Recalling the discussion in chapter one of progressivism and the problems cited in this chapter with Kohl's model, its child-centeredness may lead to a lack of structure and sufficient control, though it must be admitted that Kohl's model manifests greater concern for students than either behavior modification or assertive discipline.

Methodology and Application

The methodology and application refer to the implementation of the theory or plan. Methodology is the body of rules or procedures found in each model; application is the translation of the rules or procedures into planned activities. Although it may be assumed that both the theory, methodology, and measures for application should be equally well developed, seldom is this the case: usually one is more developed than the others. Whenever teachers are able to have favorable results in using a model that lacks a well developed theory, one is at a loss for an explanation (even if the methodology and application are well developed), because it is the theory that explains disciplinary problems and their solution. On the other hand, when the theory is well developed and the other two parts are not sufficiently developed, yet teachers still gain favorable results using the model, one would assume that either the theory is sufficiently suggestive of possible practices or teachers are using their own ingenuity in implementation.

Of the various models considered in this chapter, Kohl's Natural Development model is the least developed in terms of methodology and application. Each of the others has reasonably well explicated plans for implementation. Of these, behavior modification and Glasser's model probably would be the easiest to learn because they are clearly and simply stated and do not demand the acquisition of many new skills. But this is not the case with some of the other models. Altschuler's Social Literacy Approach would likely require supervised training and the use of specially prepared tapes; T.E.T. would require the development of more sensitive and perceptive interpersonal skills; Dreikurs' model would demand gaining a better understanding of motivational problems and observational skills to sort out what is the cause of the disruptive behavior; and assertive discipline would call for some personality changes in teachers. Thus it is likely that those models that demand special training, the relinquishing of old habits and the acquisition of new skills will less likely be adopted, other things being equal. This means that if the administration desires that teachers use one of the more demanding models, then it will likely be necessary that special workshops and training sessions be offered and incentives be given for participation. Since there are many models available, teachers and administrators have the opportunity to choose ones that will likely be successful in their school.

NOTES

1. Herbert Kohl, *On Teaching* (New York: Schocken Books, 1976), p. 100.
2. Ibid., p. 84.
3. Kohl has admitted his failures and how he profited by them in the following books: *36 Children* (New York: Signet Books, 1968) and *Half the House* (New York: Dutton, 1974).
4. Herbert Kohl, *The Open Classroom* (New York: New York Review of Books, 1969), pp. 80-81.
5. Kohl, *On Teaching*, p. 82.
6. Ibid, p. 102.
7. Thomas Gordon, *T.E.T.: Teacher Effectiveness Training* (New York: Peter H. Wyden, 1974).
8. Alfred S. Altschuler, *School Discipline: A Socially Literate Solution* (New York: McGraw-Hill, 1980).
9. See: Freire's *Pedagogy of the Oppressed* (New York: Herder and Herder, 1972); *Education for Critical Consciousness* (New York: Seabury Press, 1973); and *Education: The Practice of Freedom* (London: Writers and Readers Publishing Cooperative, 1976).
10. Altschuler, *School Discipline*, p. 84.
11. Freire, *Pedagogy of the Oppressed*, p. 40.
12. See my "Responsibility, Rights, and Accountability in Education," *The Educational Forum* 44 (March 1980):355-362.
13. William Glasser, *Reality Therapy* (New York: Harper & Row, 1965, p. 8
14. Ibid., p. 13.
15. William Glasser, *The Identity Society* (New York: Harper & Row, 1972), ch. 8; and Glasser, *Schools Without Failure* (New York: Harper & Row, 1968), ch. 2.
16. Glasser, *Schools Without Failure*, p. 201.
17. See Maslow's *Motivation and Personality*, 2nd. ed. (New York: Harper & Row, 1970).
18. See Albert Ellis, *Reason and Emotion in Psychotherapy* (New York: Lyle Stuart, 1962),

ch. 12.

19. Donald F. Shearn and Daniel Lee Randolph, "Effects of Reality Therapy Methods Applied in the Classroom," *Psychology in the Schools* (January 1978):79-83.

20. Rudolf Dreikurs, *Psychology in the Classroom*, 2nd ed. (New York: Harper & Row, 1968), p. 16.

21. Rudold Dreikurs, Bernice Brouia Grunwald, and Floy Childers Pepper, *Maintaining Sanity in Classrooms: Classroom Management Techniques*, 2nd. ed. (New York: Harper & Row, 1982), pp. 8-9.

22. Dreikurs, *Psychology*, pp. 27-32; 40-45; Dreikurs, et al., *Maintaining Sanity*, ch. 3.

23. Dreikurs, et al., *Maintaining Sanity*, pp. 126-127.

24. John B. Watson, *Psychology from the Standpoint of a Behaviorist* (Philadelphia: J. B. Lippincott, 1919).

25. Ibid., p. 10.

26. John B. Watson, *Behaviorism* (London: Kegan Paul, 1925), p. 82.

27. B. F. Skinner, *Science and Human Behavior* (New York: Macmillan, 1953), p. 258.

28. B. F. Skinner, *The Behavior of Organisms* (New York: D. Appleton-Century Co., 1938), pp. 12-13.

29. W. A. Bricker and D. D. Bricker, "Development of Receptive Vocabulary in Severely Retarded Children." *American Journal of Mental Deficiency* 74 (1970):599-607.

30. G. R. Patterson, "The Aggressive Child: Victim and Architect of a Coercive System." In E. J. Mash, L. A. Hamerlynch, and L. C. Handy (Eds.), *Behavior Modification in Families* (New York: Brunner/Mazel, 1976), pp. 267-316.

31. A. Rubin, M. Schneider, and M. Dolnick, "The Turtle Technique: An Extended Case of Self-Control in the Classroom," *Psychology in the Schools* 13 (1976):449-453.

32. H. Krop, B. Calhoon, and R. Verrier, "Modification of the 'self-concept' of Emotionally Disturbed Children by Covert Reinforcement," *Behavior Therapy* 2 (1971): 201-204.

33. Garth Blackman and Adolph Silberman, *Modification of Child and Adolescent Behavior* (Belmont, CA: Wadsworth, 1975), pp. 144-151.

34. Harold L. Cohen, "Behavior Modification and Socially Deviant Youth." In *Behavior Modification in Education*, ed. Carl E. Thoresen, 72nd Yearbook, Part I, National Society for Study of Education (Chicago: University of Chicago Press, 1972), pp. 291-314.

35. Lee Canter and Marlene Canter, *Assertive Discipline: A Take-Charge Approach for Today's Educator* (Seal Beach, CA: Canter and Associates, 1976).

36. See: Robert E. Alberti and Michael L. Emmons, *Stand Up, Speak Out, Talk Back!* (New York: Pocket Books, 1975); and Herbert Fensterheim and Jean Baer, *Don't Say Yes When You Want to Say No* (New York: Dell, 1975).

Chapter Three

CURRENT DISCIPLINARY PRACTICES
IN INNOVATIVE SCHOOLS

THOSE SCHOOLS that experienced the most serious disciplinary problems during the past decade have largely been identified and the measures they used for coping with these problems were reported.[1]

Far less explored are the schools that have the most effective and creative disciplinary programs. My hypothesis is that if a school is innovative in educational policy, organization, curriculum, instruction, or evaluation, it also will manifest effective and creative disciplinary programs. In order to test this hypothesis, a questionnaire about school disciplinary programs and policy (see Appendix) was developed and mailed to principals of 152 secondary schools identified by the U.S. Department of Education as especially innovative.[2] The questionnaire was followed up with selective interviews, both in-person and by telephone (see chapter four).

The Department of Education study of innovative schools focused on all secondary schools: high schools, junior high and middle schools. A diversity of approaches to quality education was found. Strong leadership was also identified, which confirms research findings of the positive link between leadership and the promotion of learning. The styles of leadership were diverse, ranging from the military to the cheerleader to the quiet persuader. The percentage of women principals in the schools was more than twice the national average. Other characteristics shared by these schools were a heavy emphasis on academic learning, extraordinary community support and involvement.

SCHOOL DISCIPLINE IMPROVEMENT SURVEY

The School Discipline Improvement Survey, a questionnaire, was designed to gather basic information about policy, programs, and explanations for classroom disciplinary problems. The Survey was mailed to principals of the 152 innovative schools; the number of returned questionnaires was 111, a return of 73%. Figure 3.1 shows that most of those who completed and returned the questionnaire are principals. In other cases, the assistant principal was usually given responsibility, and in only a few cases another designee. In some schools an assistant principal or another staff member is assigned chief responsibility for discipline. Let us turn now to the questions.

FIGURE 3.1

Respondent's Positions	f	%
Principals	81	(73.0)
Assistant Principals	24	(21.6)
Administrative Assistants	2	(1.8)
Dean of Students	3	(2.7)
Discipline Coordinator	1	(0.9)

1. Has you school developed a student handbook of rights and responsibilities?

    101   YES
      9   NO
      1   Parent Handbook

If the answer is YES, indicate how these rules were developed:

    25   Administration
    90   Administration and Teachers
    65   With Parent involvement
    71   With Student involvement

If the answer to Number 1 is NO, is the responsibility for classroom disciplinary rules left to each teacher?

    7   YES
    2   NO

If the answer is NO, please describe briefly how disciplinary rules are handled: It was mentioned in one response that the school district has a student code of conduct; the other response reported that Assertive Discipline is used and that rules are developed by a committee of administrators, parents, and students.

It should be noted above that in answering how the rules are developed, the figures total more than 111 (the number of returns) because some of the respondents checked more than one category (because of the wording of the question and some decentralization of policy development). The large amount of parent and student participation in developing the student handbook, as follow-up interviews indicated (see chapter four), largely took the form of consultation and feedback with the administration making final decisions. Alhough teachers were usually involved in developing the student handbook, three of the respondents indicated that rules were developed by the administration with parental and student involvement; teachers, however, were omitted.

It has been estimated that three out of every four secondary schools nationally have a printed disciplinary code.[3] In this survey of innovative schools, 91% of the schools had developed a handbook. It is assumed that it is better to have a handbook because students will know more precisely where they stand and will have a source of reference in their future behavior; moreover, teachers and administrators will have more precise guidelines for handling disciplinary problems. It is also assumed that greater compliance from students can be gained when they are consulted in developing rules of behavior, as was the practice in 64% of the innovative schools.

2. Does your school have a special program for handling difficult disciplinary problems?

- 88 YES
- 22 NO
- 1 No Reply

If the answer is YES, who is in charge of the program?

- 70 Principal and Administrative Staff
- 11 Principal
- 22 Guidance Counselor
- 23 Designated Teacher
- 15 Other

It is assumed that schools are likely to be able to cope with difficult disciplinary problems when they have established a special program for such purposes. Note that the responses exceeded the number of respondents in the follow-up question about who is in charge of the program because some respondents indicated more than one category; this type of response shows multiple sources of authority. There was a high frequency of combining Principal and Administrative Staff with either Guidance Counselor or Designated Teacher. Nevertheless, the principal and the administrative staff, not the principal alone, was the chief means for handling these programs. Of the 11 that designated that the principal is in charge of the program, three of the 11 noted that it was actually the responsibility of the vice principal. Those that indicated "Other" included such sources as dean of student services, class deans, school psychologist, person in charge of alternative program, teachers, central office, peer council, designated professional staff person, and child study team for special referrals.

3. Which model below would best describe your special program? The results are listed in the order of frequency:

FIGURE 3.2

Models of Discipline Used

40	Behavior Modification
32	Canter's Assertive Model
23	Glasser's Reality Model
17	Values Clarification
8	Gordon's Teacher Effectiveness Training
5	Engelmann and Dobson's Behavior/Punishment Model
3	Dreikurs' Social Discipline Model
0	Giott's Communication Model
0	Redl and Wattenberg's Group Management
0	Rich's Normative Proactive Discipline
24	Other

Some respondents indicated that more than one model is used in their school. Eighteen returns did not respond at all to this question, some of whom indicated that they were unfamiliar with the different models. Although Values Clarification is designed for values education programs rather than for disciplinary purposes, some schools used it, according to information gained in follow-up telephone interviews (see chapter four), to get students to think more seriously about their behavior and its causes. Some respondents indicated more than one model was used in their school; the high frequency combinations designated: Behavior Modification/Canter/Glasser; Behavior Modification/Values Clarification; Canter/Glasser. A possible explanation for the first and third combinations is that they all put the teacher in charge and are direct and forceful (as opposed to models that are more informal and less direct, such as Teacher Effectiveness Training). Glasser's Model and Behavior Modification are relatively easy to learn to use. The combination of Behavior Modification and Assertive Discipline, according to a follow-up telephone interview, was based on the conviction that Assertive Discipline is effective with typical middle class students, whereas Behavior Modification is employed in special education classes and with other students that differ from the norm.

Of the 24 who listed other approaches, the following were some of those indicated: district regulations, eclectic, no special model, peer counseling, detention hall, time-out room, in-school alternative program, removal to camp for disruptive pupils, and "old farm logic."

In order to determine the causes of classroom discipline problems and whether a consensus exists, question 4 asked: "List briefly what you believe to be three primary causes of everyday classroom discipline problems." The results were grouped under six categories and their numerical frequency is indicated.

A.	Students	111
B.	Teachers	90
C.	School	51
D.	Parents	17
E.	External Factors	22
F.	Program	13
	No response	6

The most frequently mentioned causes under each category are as follows:

A. Students

11 Low motivation/disinterest	7 Low self-concept
11 Not prepared	7 Learning disabled
9 Negative peer influence	7 Tardiness

B. Teachers

16 Classroom management skills	4 Lack of planning
15 Lack of preparation	3 Unclear expectations
7 Lack of direction and inconsistency	3 Ignorant of student knowledge
4 Lack of organization	3 Lack of empathy

Let us look at these first two categories before presenting the other four. In terms of student causes, there are few surprises other than the fact that more administrators are recognizing the influence of self-concept on behavior. Classroom management skills, not knowledge of subject matter, is perceived as the single most important cause in terms of teacher behavior. But it could also be noted that lack of empathy and insufficient knowledge of students are also recognized as causes.

C. *School Organization:*

12 Lack of clear rules and
   expectations
 6 Ineffective communication
 6 Lack of consistent enforcement

 3 Personality clashes
 3 Poor planning
 3 Size of classes
 2 Lack of administrative support

F. *Program:*
 3 Lack of relevant interest
 2 Lack of student success with
   program
 1 Lack of materials

D. *Parents*

13 Lack of parental support and
   understanding
 7 Lack of appropriate parenting
 2 Negative parent/student
   attitudes
 1 Lack of involvement

E. *External Factors:*
10 Home problems
 2 Community disputes
 2 Society's failure to motivate
 2 Weather

Looking at the last three categories, it can be observed that administrators recognize and are willing to assume some of the responsibility for the causes of classroom discipline problems. But whether theirs is a critique of their own adminisration or others they have observed is unclear; nevertheless, it does show the importance of better school organization, especially the development of clear rules and expectations.

In looking at the parental role, it is not unexpected that a lack of parental support and understanding would lead the list; yet since only one respondent indicated a lack of parental involvement as a cause, the problem of support and understanding stems less from uninvolvement than from probably inadequate communication or a clash of values. As for external factors, not only home problems but community disputes and society's failure to motivate are seen as problems.

Programmatic and curricular causes of discipline problems were identified, but surprisingly, were not seen as significant or influential as other causes despite the fact that ever since progressive education the curriculum has been cited as one of the most important influences on student attitudes and interests. Respondents suggest that the teacher's instructional planning and classroom management are more significant influences than curriculum content on everyday classroom disciplinary problems.

The fourth and last question asked that the respondent indicate those areas where your school has developed written policies or rules regulating student behavior. The responses are listed below in numerical sequence rather than the order in which they appeared on the questionnaire.

FIGURE 3.3

Number of Schools with Written Behavioral Rules

110	Attendance
108	Drugs
107	Alcohol
105	Suspension and explusion
103	Smoking and tobacco
101	Fighting
96	Student records
93	Due process
86	Vandalism and/or theft
85	Detention
83	Search and seizure for illegal items
83	Physical assault on school personnel
82	Physical assault on students
76	Corporal punishment
72	Trespassing
71	Extortion and intimidation
71	Dress code
70	Bomb threats
68	Cheating
67	Gambling
65	Parent-teacher & parent-administrator discipline conferences
60	Coordination of discipline action with guidance and counseling
57	Student grievance procedures
57	Law enforcement officers in the school
53	Forgery
51	Misdemeanor/felonies
47	Student participation in developing school rules
42	Interrogation
39	Parent liability for their children's vandalism
13	Student disciplinary committee
13	Other

Of the Other responses, two pertained to tardiness to class; some responses related to state, county, or district policies; still others mentioned medication taken at school, Saturday work detail, in-school suspension, class cutting, athletic/extra-curricular eligibility, failure to do homework, and failure to read during "sustained silent reading time."

One need not assume that the high incidence of a policy in a particular area necessarily indicates that schools have had considerable problems in that area. For instance, cheating is virtually universal and can even be found in military academies with honor codes; and although it may not be widespread in some schools, only 61 percent of the schools have established a policy in this area. On the other hand, most all schools have regulations governing the use of drugs and alcohol; but, according to follow-up interviews, this does not mean that innovative schools have considerable problems in these areas. Regulations are developed in some cases to anticipate the types of problems that may arise and thereby to discourage undesirable activities and to control them should they arise. The large number of schools that have rules governing student records (96) and due process (93) may stem from a need to coordinate school policies with federal legislation and court decisions in these areas.

In conclusion, it would appear that schools selected as innovative on criteria other than disciplinary policy, manifest certain innovative tendencies in the latter area as well. The criteria for innovative schools as developed by the U.S. Department of Education is accepted here; in addition, though innovative policies may be diverse, they would differ from such traditional models as Calvinism, militarism, and essentialism (see chapter one).

A larger percentage of innovative secondary schools (91%) have a handbook or disciplinary code than the national average of secondary schools (75%). Other comparative figures are not available, but it should be noted the widespread participation by teachers, parents, and students in developing a student handbook of rights and responsibilities. It is also assumed that students will more likely comply with regulations when they are consulted in the process of developing them.

In their response to the causes of classroom disciplinary problems, the respondents did not resort to a few simple, overworked explanations: "spare the rod and spoil the child," laziness, lack of respect for teachers, and the like. Instead, a surprising multiplicty of explanations were offered stemming from six major areas. The ability to recognize the complexity of disciplinary problems, the involvement of groups other than the administration in developing student handbooks, and the willingness to try out different models of classroom discipline all suggest innovative approaches to school discipline.

NOTES

1. National Institute of Education, *Violent Schools — Safe Schools: The Safe School Report to Congress*, vol. 1 (Washington, D.C.: Government Printing Office, 1978).
2. T. H. Bell, "America Can Do it," *American Education* 19 (December 1983):4-9.
3. D. Safer, *School Programs for Disruptive Adolescents* (Baltimore: University Park Press, 1982).

Chapter Four

PRINCIPALS' VIEWS OF
SCHOOL DISCIPLINARY POLICY

THE RESULTS of the questionnaire provided basic data about discipline in innovative secondary schools. Yet it did not explain the procedures used in developing and enforcing school disciplinary policy, special problems encountered in administering the policy, the reactions and effect of policy on students and teachers, and other questions dealing with day-to-day operations of school discipline.

Visitations were made to selected schools for in-depth interviews with those in charge of disciplinary policy in order to supplement the questionnaires;. and where travel costs were prohibitive, telephone interviews were conducted.

The interviews initially sought to uncover the locus of authority for school discipline; how discipline is related to organized instruction; the influence of student handbooks of rights and responsibilities on behavior; whether disciplinary policies are derived from school goals, a written statement of educational philosophy, or other sources; the results achieved in those schools that officially adopted a model or theory of discipline; and how new legal provisions for the handicapped and student due process rights have affected disciplinary policies. As the interviews proceeded, however, it was found that either some of these areas were less important than expected, or that sufficient information was unavailable; moreover, as the interviews unfolded, some unanticipated lines of fruitful inquiry were suggested. As a consequence, the structure of the interviews took a somewhat different shape than originally anticipated.

THE LOCUS OF DISCIPLINARY POLICY
AND ITS ENFORCEMENT

The questionnaire revealed that in a majority of cases the student handbook of rights and responsibilities was not developed exclusively by the administration but involved participation by either teachers, parents, or students, or a combination of these groups. The interviews sought to determine, whenever other groups were involved, how they were involved and what procedures were followed.

At Lee County Senior High School in Sanford, North Carolina, the principal initially developed the handbook; when it was time to revise it, he appointed a committee consisting of nine parents, nine teachers, and nine students that met twice each year.[1] Student body officers were members of the panel at Soldotna High School, Soldotna, Alaska, to develop a student handbook, with an active parental advisory committee.[2] Some schools are legally required to initiate certain forms of participation. At Spartanburg High School in Spartanburg, South Carolina, it is mandatory to have a School Improvement Council that serves to suggest policy to the Board of Education. The Council is composed of principals, faculty, students, and parents.[3] A School Site Council was developed at Venado Middle School in Irvine, California, which is composed of parent representatives and the Student Council; the group meets monthly and provides input to the administration.[4] A variation is found at York Community High School in Elmhurst, Illinois, where student government has an advisory committee on rights and responsibilities and the PTA has an advisory committee on student conduct, and the latter group can communicate its suggestions to the Board of Education.[5] Another plan is to create advisory groups of students for representation and counseling purposes. Each advisory group of 2-5 students is determined by the administration and faculty at Cashmere Middle School, Cashmere, Washington; each advisory group elects one representative to the Student Council, which will make suggestions to the administration as to what rules would be acceptable to their peers.[6]

How do innovative secondary schools surveyed handle persistent and difficult problems? In other words, when a teacher is continuing to have problems with a student that he or she feels unable to handle, what are the next steps available to the teacher? Most of the principals have developed guidelines for handling school situations; these guidelines, in many cases, involved a series of steps in case the problem behavior has not been rectified after the first step.

The first step in some schools is to refer the offender to the principal's office; in other schools intermediate steps may be used. At Rhodes Junior High School in Mesa, Arizona, the teacher has three options: notify the parents, work with the counselor, or involve the administration. In the latter case, for certain offenses — abusive language and insubordination — the student would be sent to the principal.[7] In more serious cases, a few schools, such as Shue Middle School, in Newark, Delaware, may refer the student to an alternative learning center.[8] A particular principal may be designated to handle referrals. At Stephen F. Austin High School in Austin, Texas, an associate principal handles referrals and an assistant principal supervises attendance.[9] But in some schools the principal may use intermediaries to work with the teacher, such as at Willis Junior High School in Chandler, Arizona, a master teacher and the department chairperson are available, as part of a building management team, to work with teachers on discipline and other problems.[10]

A teacher may fill out a referral form and the student will be sent to the principal's office; the student might then be placed in a "time-out" or detention room. At Hoover Middle School in Albuquerque, New Mexico, the student signs a contract as to his goals and conduct; the student, however, could remain indefinitely in the time-out room until he or she is willing to change behavior by fulfilling an acceptable contract; those who refuse to live up to the contract would be suspended.[11] An option in one school district is to have the detention at a Saturday School, as an alternative to out-of-school suspension.[12]

How the principal will handle the problem and the penalties involved would depend upon the circumstances and the seriousness of the offense. Fighting, use of drugs, alcohol, obscenities, and disrespect to faculty are usually considered more serious offenses. At Albuquerque High School in Albuquerque, New Mexico, the parent will be called and the student may be suspended; for the second offense, the student could be suspended for a semester.[13] Expulsion in most school districts is handled by the school board using full due process proceedings. Where in many schools out-of-school suspension may be for as short a time as three days, expulsion could be for a semester, the remainder of the school year, or permanently.

MODELS OF DISCIPLINE

As noted from the questionnaire findings, the most popular disciplinary models used in the classroom are behavior modification, assertive discipline, and values clarification (in that order). Some schools have adopted no particular model; others have a school-wide model that teachers are encouraged to use; and still others have adopted more than one model.

In schools that have adopted one model, it was reported at Hoover Middle School that many teachers do not like Glasser's model because it is too time consuming, not adult enough in how students are approached, and the school is handicapped because the district does not provide a time-out room.[14] One school that used Dreikurs' model left it up to each teacher but found that it has not as yet been "put together well."[15] Behavior modification is used at Mt. Ararat School in Topsham, Maine, but is employed mostly in special education classes.[16] Behavior modification is used, but not mandated, at Spartanburg High School, Spartanburg, South Carolina, and some "small gains" have been registered.[17] Through in-service training teachers learn the techniques and skills needed for handling this model. At Lakewood Junior High in Luling, Louisiana, teachers were reported "very comfortable" with assertive discipline, but have found that they must "be consistent" in handling the plan.[18]

Why do some schools use more than one disciplinary model? At Lee County Senior High School in Sanford, North Carolina, there would be no way with 115 teachers, according to the principal, that one model could be suitable for all; consequently, through workshops three models are available (behavior modification, assertive discipline, and Glasser's model), even though the principal concluded that assertive discipline is "by far the most effective."[19] South Eugene High School in Eugene, Oregon, uses Dreikurs' model and Teacher Effectiveness Training; these are viewed as "resources that teachers could tap into" by permitting each teacher to choose the model preferred.[20]

CLASS SIZE, INSTRUCTION, AND DISCIPLINE

Of 24 interviews, 11 respondents held that there is a positive relationship between the rise of disciplinary problems and class size; eight respondents found no relationship; two respondents stated that all their classes are of certain size (therefore, they ventured no judgment); and three did not respond to the question.[21] Most who denied that a positive relationship exists made no further comment about it; those few who elaborated their ideas on this point held that discipline problems depended upon the teacher's classroom management rather than class size. Of those who discerned a positive correlation, some mentioned that a class above 25 students may create problems.[22]

What relationship, if any, exists between instruction and discipline? In other words, do those teachers who plan instruction well and teach effectively have less discipline problems? Most principals observed that students perform for well-prepared teachers, that good instructional planning lowers discipline problems, and the ability to actively involve most students most of the time decreases disruptive behavior.

And what is being done to recruit teachers who possess these and related characteristics? One principal noted that those teachers who handle discipline well have a knowledge of their students, knowledge of oneself, a sense of humor, energy, and are happy with their profession.[23] Some seek teachers who are well organized and consistent in working with students;[24] some look for teachers willing to get involved in extracurricular activities;[25] and still others try to recruit teachers who love kids and know their subject.[26] In interviews, some principals would inquire how the prospective teacher would handle classroom management and their relations with parents;[27] some would be interested in whether the teacher could set up rules and follow through on them.[28] Principals are aided in recruitment in some districts by prescreening of candidates at the district level.[29]

Are there more discipline problems according to age or grade level? Here the response naturally varied because the sample included junior high, middle schools, and senior high schools. No consensus was reached, but the eighth, ninth, and tenth grades were mentioned the most frequently as having problems. For those few principals who attempted to explain the concentration of problems at certain grades, one said that the eighth and ninth grades are "just the age students are trying to find themselves."[30] A senior high principal observed that because of immaturity and problems of identity, ninth graders "had to break all rules at least once."[31]

CONCLUSIONS

In retrospect, most innovative secondary schools have well-defined plans for handling disciplinary problems and have disseminated a set of rules for handling various types of cases. Plans are not merely for dealing with cases after they occur but to establish an environment for preventing problems from arising and to create better conditions for learning. Some schools have experimented with different models and, in some instances, held workshops to help teachers learn to utilize these models.

Procedures for handling difficult and persistent disciplinary problems vary but may likely be referred to the administration when intermediate procedures are unsuccessful. Some administrators prefer to see teachers try to work out the problem themselves and, if unsuccessful, they might call in the parents, talk to a master teacher or to a counselor about the problem; other administrators have the teacher refer the problem sooner to a designated principal. Most schools use some form of in-school detention before resorting to out-of-school suspension. In the more serious cases, out-of-school suspension for varying time periods are used (depending upon the offense), and only in exceptional cases do school boards have to resort to expulsion. In York Community High School in Elmhurst, Illinois, a police officer in civilian clothes talks with students and parents about criminal trespassing, vandalism, drugs, and related matters.[32] Albuquerque, New Mexico, public schools instituted a program in the 1970-71 academic year in which the police, community, and the schools work together for the benefit of the children. At first, opposition was expressed because other agencies would know about school problems, but today, with eight detectives assigned to the schools to handle drugs, thefts, assaults, weapons, and other unlawful activity, the program is more widely accepted.[33]

Overall, despite both the Reagan administration and the public's concerns about discipline problems, the situation nationally is better than the early 1970s. As one principal observed, disciplinary problems peaked in the early 1970s; the situation is now similar to the 1960s.[34] This view is supported by the "Safe School Study" that showed violence increased from the early sixties to the seventies but leveled off after the early 1970s.[35] Despite these improvements, the innovative schools surveyed were not complacent, and many were experimental and receptive to new ideas. What we must do now was aptly expressed by a principal: "Be well prepared. And be friendly, fair, and firm."[36]

NOTES

1. C. W. Seagraves, Principal, Lee County Senior High School, Sanford, North Carolina (Telephone interview, December 12, 1984).
2. Frank C. Garrity, Assistant Principal, Soldotna High School, Soldotna, Alaska (Telephone interview, December 11, 1984).
3. Albert L. Jeter, Assistant Principal, Spartanburg High School, Spartanburg, South Carolina (Telephone interview, December 5, 1984).
4. John D. Tennant, Principal, Venado Middle School, Irvine, California (Telephone interview, December 4, 1984).
5. James W. Nelson, Principal, York Community High School, Elmhurst, Illinois (Telephone interview, November 30, 1984).
6. Ed Tuggle, Principal, Cashmere Middle School, Cashmere, Washington (Telephone interview, November 29, 1984).

7. Dan E. Young, Principal, Rhodes Junior High School, Mesa, Arizona (Telephone interview, December 13, 1984).

8. Richard E. Williams, Assistant Principal, Shue Middle School, Newark, Delaware (Telephone interview, November 28, 1984).

9. Jacquelyn McGee, Principal, and Jack Kinkel, Associate Principal, Stephen F. Austin High School, Austin, Texas (In-person interview, October 23, 1984).

10. Dale Hancock, Principal, Willis Junior High School, Chandler, Arizona (Telephone interview, December 10, 1984).

11. John Garrison, Principal, Hoover Middle School, Albuquerque, New Mexico (In-person interview, November 15, 1984).

12. Judy Wayland, Principal, Renne Intermediate, Newberg, Oregon (Telephone interview, December 14, 1984).

13. George Bello, Principal, Albuquerque High School, Albuquerque, New Mexico (In-person interview, November 16, 1984).

14. Garrison (November 15, 1984).

15. Tuggle (November 29, 1984).

16. Ashley LeBlanc, Assistant Principal, Mt. Ararat School, Topsham, Maine (Telephone interview, November 30, 1984)

17. Jeter (December 5, 1984).

18. John C. Walker, Principal, Lakewood Junior High School, Luling, Louisiana (Telephone interview, December 6, 1984).

19. Seagraves (December 12, 1984).

20. Wayne P. Hill, Assistant Principal, South Eugene High School, Eugene, Oregon (Telephone interview, November 28, 1984).

21. The reason for no response from three interviewees was that in one case (in interviewing a detective assigned to the school district) the question was not germane; in the other two instances the interviewer overlooked raising the question.

22. Gary F. Hodgson, Principal, West Ottawa Middle School, Holland, Michigan (Telephone interview, November 28, 1984); and Robert C. Sell, Associate Principal, Welton High School, Welton, Connecticut (Telephone interview, December 5, 1984).

23. Shelby Copland, Assistant Principal, Hoover Middle School, Albuquerque, New Mexico (In-person interview, November 15, 1984).

24. Irene Horner, Associate Principal, Churchill High School, San Antonio, Texas (In-person interview, October 26, 1984).

25. Bello (November 16, 1984).

26. Jo Ann Kreuger, Principal, Monzano High School, Albuquerque, New Mexico (In-person interview, November 15, 1984).

27. John D. Tennant, Principal, Venado Middle School, Venado, California (Telephone interview, December 4, 1984).

28. Helen Nash, Assistant Principal, Hanford Secondary School, Richland, Washington (Telephone interview, December 3, 1984).

29. Young (December 13, 1984).

30. Nash (December 3, 1984).

31. Seagraves (December 12, 1984).

32. Nelson (November 30, 1984).

33. Bob Milliman, Detective, Monzano High School, Albuquerque, New Mexico

(In-person interview, November 15, 1984).

34. Krueger (November 15, 1984).
35. National Institute of Education, Violent Schools — Safe Schools: The Safe Study Report to Congress, vol. 1 (Washington, D.C.: Government Printing Office, 1978), pp. 1-14.
36. Seagraves (December 12, 1984).

Chapter Five

AN ASSESSMENT OF SCHOOL DISCIPLINE

A GROWING research literature has provided valuable leads as to how schools, as social and educational systems, can provide an environment where effective discipline is the norm. These studies grew rapidly during the late 1960s and early 1970s when problems of disruption and violence in American schools reached their peak.

This chapter will explore a number of significant topics that illuminate school discipline from fresh perspectives. Recent research on effective schools shows that schools can make a difference in student achievement and other aspects of student growth. A number of salient characteristics have been identified as contributing to effective schools; among them is good discipline and an orderly environment for learning.

Effective schools have well conceived policies. In order to develop sound policy, it is necessary, first of all, to understand its nature and characteristics; next, the stages of policy development need to be understood. Four stages of policy development are presented along with their distinctive characteristics and problems.

In some schools where policy breaks down and untoward events occur, schools no longer are safe because of the dangers of violence, vandalism, drug use, and related problems. A number of promising measures are presented for creating safe schools that promote a more desirable learning environment. The relative effectiveness of these different measures are assessed.

Lately researchers have focused on classroom management as a way to improve learning and promote discipline. This topic concerns what teachers can do in the way of preparation and planning to enhance classroom activities; it does not deal with discipline problems outside the classroom, but it offers valuable guidelines for improving teacher planning and procedures.

GOVERNANCE, DISCIPLINARY POLICY, AND EFFECTIVE SCHOOLS

Recent literature on school effectiveness shows that schools do affect students' academic achievement. This literature challenges earlier studies that found unequal academic achievement a function of family background.[1] Does this literature have any bearing on discipline or is it limited to achievement test scores?

Judging from interview results in chapter four, instructional effectiveness has a direct bearing on discipline. Most secondary school principals reported that sound instructional planning lowers discipline problems, and the ability to involve students decreases disruptive behavior.

Research on effective schools, therefore, may illuminate the relationship between discipline and sound instructional planning. According to this research, the following school-level characteristics promote higher achievement in basic skills: First, a school climate that is conducive to learning — it is free from disciplinary problems and embodies high expectations for student achievement. Second, a schoolwide emphasis on basic skills. Third, the development of a system of clear instructional objectives for monitoring and assessing students' performance. Finally, a school principal who is a strong programmatic leader, sets high standards, frequently observes classrooms, and creates learning incentives.[2] The elements of school effectiveness must be considered in relationship to all the other elements and in terms of the situation in which found; they cannot meaningfully be considered in isolation from one another.

But researchers do not know whether these characteristics are the cause of school effectiveness; nor have these characteristics been ranked in importance. Evidently these multiple characteristics in combination with one another would need to be implemented to ensure desired results.

Since the characteristics above are related to success in imparting basic skills, the characteristics of effective schools are stated somewhat differently: (1) the principal's leadership ability and emphasis on the quality of instruction; (2) a broad and pervasive instructional focus; (3) a safe, orderly climate conducive to teaching and learning; (4) teachers who promote at least minimum mastery; and (5) program evaluation based on measures of student achievement.[3]

Other studies of school effectiveness, especially with an emphasis on program evaluation, agreed with many of the five characteristics above but also mentioned high staff morale and expectations; a high degree of staff control over instructional and training decisions; and clear goals for the school. Once again, two characteristics previously listed are clear leadership from the principal and a sense of order in the school.[4]

An example of some of the more promising investigations of school effectiveness is the longitudinal study conducted by Rutter and others.[5] The study examined 12 inner-city secondary schools in London in terms of students' in-school behavior, attendance, examination success, and delinquency. It was found that scholastic achievement is affected by the school attended but less affected by school size, age of building or space available. Thus, good outcomes can be obtained despite unpromising school premises. Effective schools were brought about by, among other things, teachers who prepared lessons in advance, were punctual, and directed attention to the class as a whole. Students had better school success when homework was regularly assigned and graded, and when told that they are capable of learning and will learn.

In summarizing school effectiveness studies, it has been found that "schools, particularly at the secondary level, make a difference in subject-specific instruction. Further, this difference is to a large extent independent of home background and is related to structure, discipline, homework, and general press to achieve in school."[6] Additionally, in light of the importance of the principal's leadership as a characteristic of effective schools and the role of the principal in the development, dissemination, and implementation of such policy, it is essential that closer attention be given this vital area.

Policy Characteristics and Development

Policy serves several functions. It serves to regulate institutions and organizations; it provides orderly guidelines for day-to-day operations and thereby affords a sense of continuity. Policy also specifies guidelines to govern the introduction and application of innovations within organizational systems. Policy is also used to specify the allocation of funds and resources to a project, and to state what is prescribed, prohibited, or permitted in a social system. For personnel, policy provides a set of expectations and directives that partly define the individual's performance of roles in an organization. Policy can also create and define the activities of an educational institution. It can lead to a change in educational institutions.

Policy is a form of rule. A distinction, however, can be made here between the rules of natural languages, such as English, and the rules of an organization. The rules of natural languages must be found rather than made up; it is a matter of empirical confirmation to discover what rules do in fact guide the linguistic behavior of certain people. In contrast, the rules of organizations and educational systems are created.

A rule is a type of generalization used to prescribe conduct, action, or usage. A distinction can be made between regulative and constitutive rules.[7] Regulative rules require antecedents or independently existing forms of behavior. Constitutive rules not only regulate but also create or define new forms of behavior. Etiquette would be an example of regulative rules; sports or games, such as football or chess, are examples of constitutive rules because the rules make possible the playing of such sports or games. In other words, constitutive rules create the games, whereas regulative rules control preexisting forms of behavior.

Most school or classroom disciplinary rules are regulative in the sense that they regulate antecedent or independently existing forms of behavior. Student handbooks would be an example of regulative rules. When a school or a teacher adopts a new model of discipline it may be a case of constitutive rules being employed. For instance, suppose a teacher who formerly used behavior modification in class substitutes for it Altschuler's Social Literacy Approach. The two models, as will be recalled from chapter two, differ greatly. The latter model would redefine what is meant by discipline and the way that school situations should be reinterpreted in light of exercises to facilitate consciousness-raising — that an innovation counts as a policy within certain contexts, and that, in the context, there is nothing preexistent to regulate means that the innovation is an example of a constitutive rule. In this case, the adoption of the Social Literacy Approach would introduce constitutive rules in the classroom; nevertheless, teachers and students would still be expected to abide by the regulative rules that govern teachers' professional performance and student behavior.

Policy brings under rule decision, behavior which is of concern to institutions. Rules justify themselves in experience when they help to secure a desired end and do so efficiently. For instance, rule A is preferred to B in order to achieve end E if A can achieve E more efficiently and not create disorderly behavior but create such resentment among students affected that they may clandestinely seek to subvert other rules or various school or classroom activities; hence, the rule should be discarded, even if more efficient, because it is counterproductive.

By following a rule one's action is said to be rule-governed. Rule-governed behavior can be thought of as rational in the sense that reasons can be offered; reasons can be given for abiding by a rule in terms of its ability to achieve the desired end and its efficacy in doing so. Dispute at this point could arise over whether the claims for the rule can be supported. The dispute is settled by reference to authoritative case studies which demonstrate that following the rule achieves the stated objectives.

Another type of dispute is where the ends which rule-following is designed to fulfill are questioned. The question of the appropriateness of the rules and reasonableness of following them is put aside until the question of ends is successfully adjudicated.

When policymaking is undergirded by general norms, it provides a broader context for its development. General norms emerge from a culture's value system and serve as moral principles and ideals by means of which the general rules of conduct are constructed. General norms are universal and noncontextual in scope insofar as they apply to persons in various situations and circumstances. A prohibition against murder applies to everyone. Policies, in contrast, are context dependent because they regulate the activities of a particular institution or subunit of the institution at a particular time and place and apply only to persons who come under the framework of the policy network.

Let us turn now to the stages of school disciplinary policy development. The stages of policy development are: formulation, dissemination, implementation, and evaluation. Among the sources for policy formulation are educational philosophy, science, value systems, educational aims, educational standards, public opinion, and futuristic studies. Each of these has certain strengths and limitations.

A philosophy of education would contain a value system, educational aims, standards, perhaps certain scientific findings about education, and other features. To the extent that these elements provide a source or grounding for policy, then this would be a fruitful source. In practice, however, many schools have not identified exclusively with a single philosophy and would therefore need to look elsewhere for an acceptable source.

Science could provide authoritative findings about the conditions of education but would not prescribe what should be done; consequently, scientific findings could help prevent policy makers from developing policies that educators could not fulfill. In other words, if scientific findings show that because of limitations in human abilities a certain policy is too demanding for most teachers to fulfill, then the policy would have to be rejected as unrealistic and unreasonable. Science could also show what policies are likely to be implemented effectively; among those, it would not prescribe which ones to choose.

Value systems would be a fruitful source if a consensus could be reached as to what value system to adopt. Since a number of value systems may be represented in the larger community, can one value system be designated as a guide without evoking considerable controversy and conflict? One solution may be to utilize a democratic value system; even here, however, such democratic principles as freedom, equality, and justice are open to divergent interpretations. Nevertheless, there is no reason why a plausible interpretation cannot be chosen and defended.

Although educational aims are frequently contested, if a consensus on aims could be reached, then one test for policy is the extent to which it would help realize the school's aims or goals. Policy would also determine the means and measures for achieving the goals. For instance, if one goal is for students to learn to respect duly constituted authority, then school policies would regulate how instructional and socialization processes are to be conducted to achieve this end.

Educational standards, on the other hand, are measures to inform us about the success of policy in achieving goals. Policy, for example, would establish a school evaluation program and as to how it should be administered; the internal standards of the evaluation program are measures for ascertaining the achievement level of students and, as a consequence, how well certain school goals are being fulfilled.

Public opinion can never be ignored by public institutions. It is still incumbent upon professional educators, however, to evaluate public opinion in light of educational research findings and the goals of the school system in order to arrive at an independent decision which, if it differs from public opinion, will need to be defended by re-educating the public by means of authoritative findings and rational persuasion.

Futuristic studies are valuable for policy-makers because policy is not merely for the moment but must be based on long-term planning. The difficulty with futuristic studies, despite some improvements in forecasting, is that many future scenarios are still highly speculative or involve merely projections of present trends (which may be fallacious if unexpected events occur in the near future). In any case, whatever future trends are observed as a basis for policy planning, the significance of these trends will still need to be considered in light of a value system or the school's goals before definite policy decisions are made. Administrators, for example, may be informed that in the next five years a much larger percentage of students from minority backgrounds will be enrolled in their school district. Policies adopted may depend upon the system's goals and its interpretation of the principle of equality.

Once general decisions are made as to the types of policies needed, the matter of formulation arises. The scope of policy statements range from highly general to very specific; in some instances the term "policy" is used for the former type and the term "rules" for the latter type. A schoolwide statement that "Equal consideration will be given to all students in hearings to assess penalties in disciplinary cases" would be an example of a school policy; whereas, "Students are expected to clean up all trash around their desk before being dismissed" is an example of a classroom rule. Specific rules offer the advantage of clarity and unambiguity as to what behaviors are expected; the disadvantage, however, is that highly specific rules of limited scope may encourage teachers to proliferate classroom rules and thereby impart a coercive atmosphere that impedes learning. In contrast, the general terms used to formulate policies provide flexibility and adaptability to changing situations; yet such general formulations may render the policy susceptible to limited or distorted interpretations. But the very fact that some policies must be written to cover multiple and even unpredictable situations renders it essential that policy statements be formulated in sufficiently broad and flexible terms.

A set of policies needs to be disseminated to all those whose behavior will be affected by the policies. Whenever new policies are complex or require new ways of behavior, it is necessary to lay the groundwork for such changes through conferences, discussions, workshops, and other measures. In adopting a new model of classroom discipline school-wide, teachers should be involved in the decision process and be given assistance in learning the proposed techniques by providing for workshops or special classes.

New policies may also clash with pockets of vested interests; therefore, policy-makers must anticipate resistance to change in order to overcome, compensate for, or pacify these forces. In other cases, it may be necessary to interpret complex and far-reaching policy decisions by a series of guidelines which make explicit the steps needed to execute policy. Thus, in the dissemination stage the policy-maker must anticipate and evaluate a host of factors prior to deciding on the proper course of action: the complexity of policy changes, the degree to which policy departs from past practices, the ability of personnel to execute policy successfully, and the possible conflict of the policy with vested interests.

Policies cannot be successfully implemented when personnel are not adequately informed or when they fail to understand their role in policy implementation. Implementing policy can be better understood in terms of its effect on organizational roles. To implement policy successfully, it is first necessary for personnel to reconceptualize their role by internalizing their new responsibilities and relating them to previous ones. One not only needs to apprehend the meaning of the new policy and its ramifications but also to determine the types of action most likely to fulfill the policy. Standards of successful performance are needed to guide conduct and make evaluations.

One type of evaluation is by means of a general system approach, which would attempt to determine the new output of a system by ascertaining inputs and outputs and the extent to which output exceeds input. There are many problems in conducting such an evaluation where products are produced; the problems are multiplied in school systems where no product is involved and unanimity is sometimes lacking on what should constitute outputs and how they should be measured. Intangible outputs are difficult to measure and therefore more readily measurable factors are commonly employed, such as achievement-test scores. In other cases, where it is recognized that longitudinal studies of graduates are needed, costs and the ability of school systems to successfully conduct such studies impose serious limitations.

Evaluation is not limited to the terminal stage of the policy process but occurs in some form, if conducted correctly, at each stage of the policy-development process; if this were not undertaken, unwise decisions could not be rescinded at any particular point in the process. Evaluation is the first step in improving policy. After the findings are interpreted, the policy-maker must determine their significance and how they will be used to change the policy process. In conclusion, careful attention to all stages of policy development—formulation, dissemination, implementation, and evaluation—is needed for the improvement of educational policy.

CREATING SAFE SCHOOLS

All schools have some form of policy; some schools, however, give careful attention to policy development while others do not; still other schools may in effect require teachers and students to infer policy from sanctions imposed for various offenses. In other words, if rules governing student absenteeism are unclear, it may be necessary to see what are the sanctions and whether they are promptly and fairly enforced. Policies, in some instances, may be clearly defined and in place but inadequate to cope with changing conditions, as when the composition of a school's student population changes rapidly with a large influx of students from different socioeconomic and ethnic groups. Of course, many problems of disruption cannot be ascribed to policy problems: problems lie in breakdown in other aspects of school systems and in the unresolved social problems of communities.

Some schools, especially during the early 1970s, were unable to maintain a safe environment and were confronted with the problem of reestablishing control in order to overcome serious outbreaks of disruption and violence. Control in itself is not discipline if by discipline one means that student agency must be involved; i.e., student free will to bring about self-discipline. When educators use coercion or power, such use cannot be considered discipline because student agency is bypassed; yet these measures may be necessary to restore order where disruption is widespread and personal safety is endangered.

Although the most serious school offenses peaked nationwide in the mid-seventies, the problem is still serious in a minority of school districts; moreover, those educators in schools where a relatively safe environment prevails would like to maintain and even improve that environment. As late as 1978, the National Institute of Education's "Safe School Study" still found around 6,700 schools seriously affected by crime.[8] Not only the disruptions and the dangers of physical harm and property damage are threats in some schools but, as a consequence, fear rises and precludes a healthy learning environment. The Study found that 20 percent of the students were sometimes afraid of being hurt, while 3 percent said they were afraid most of the time. This meant that these students avoided restrooms and other places in school where they anticipated danger. Moreover, 12 percent of the teachers, some 120,000, hesitated to confront misbehaving students.[9]

Teachers need the cooperation of school administrators in disciplining and suspending violent students and for preparing official reports of assaults on teachers; otherwise, teacher morale will be low, some teachers will seek to transfer to another school (which their principal may not permit), and still others will drop out of teaching altogether. A psychiatrist's evaluation of 575 teachers referred to him between 1972 and 1979 suffering extraordinary and continuing stress bore a striking resemblance to "combat neurosis" among the psychiatric casualties of World War II. Many of these teachers had unconsciously expected their students to see them as wise parental figures and could not understand why violence was directed at them.[10]

It is insufficient for a teacher to have skills in using one of the contemporary models of discipline (presented in chapter two) if the school is unsafe, as these models are largely strategies for coping with everyday classroom discipline problems rather than the most serious problems of drugs, weapons, violence, and vandalism. Hence it behooves the school board to devise policies and sanctions that will restore order and create a safe school environment.

The most seriously affected schools have tried a host of measures: security guards, undercover police, electronic-alarm systems, electronic surveillance, guard dogs, architecturally redesigned schools to reduce vandalism and theft, paid community security aides, and voluntary security help.[11]

Apart from the relative effectiveness of the different measures to reduce violence and vandalism, what principles should be observed before adopting of any security measure? Assuming that disruptions are sufficiently serious to warrant considering these measures, any measures used should not violate the rights of students, teachers, and other personnel. Some electronic devices may invade students' privacy. Security guards or police, when quelling violence, should not use violence except when unavoidable. Security measures should be applied fairly and equitably. For instance, standards should not be applied unevenly so that minorities are more likely to be apprehended or singled out as disrupters or, when apprehended, given more severe penalities than other students.

Many architectural and building changes may prove effective in reducing theft and vandalism without violating any of the principles stated above: new multistrength windows that have many times the strength of regular glass, electronic-alarm systems, changes to reduce vandalism (roofs with plastic domes instead of skylights, bricking up openings in storerooms and basements that have an entry problem, more sophisticated door and window hardware, and so on).

Assigning police or security guards may create more problems than it solves. The constant presence of uniformed and armed police can create friction with students, most police are not specially trained to work with youth, and the stationing of police in school presents an image of an armed camp. When security guards are employed in schools, they should be identifiable but not wear police uniforms; they should have special training, as do detectives assigned to Albuquerque Public Schools (see chapter four), in psychology and human relations so they can work effectively with students, faculty, and parents. It is best to employ specially trained security guards without guns and to establish a functional liaison between the local chief of police and the principal.[12] In a survey of school districts with more than 10,000 students, it was found that less than half of the school districts that employ security officers have a formal training program and that most of the training is on the job.[13]

Guard dogs to intercept vandals and uncover drugs may pose problems of invading privacy, may give the school district a bad image, and could cause liability problems if they interfere with persons not linked to an offense. Whether to use community aides and volunteers would depend upon the tasks assigned them and their qualifications.

Roving gangs pose a threat in some school districts. Since most gangs are of school age, they may be found in school areas for purposes of recruitment, sharing information, and planning activities. A conservative estimate is that gangs are responsible for more than half of the vandalism in Los Angeles schools.[14] The activities of gangs on school grounds create a climate of fear that reduces school attendance and inhibits learning. In Philadelphia a coordinated program has brought gang activity under control by involving school officials, community leaders, churches, recreational centers, neighborhood crisis-intervention teams, and informal parents' councils.[15] Thus school officials need to solicit the cooperation and support of key persons and appropriate agencies in the larger society to help control this problem and other ones that affect schools but have their origin mainly in the larger society.

School size is a significant variable because smaller schools pose fewer security hazards than larger ones. Although larger schools are somewhat less expensive to construct on a per-pupil basis, the savings may be negated by the greater amount of vandalism in the larger schools. As schools and classes grow in size, teachers have more difficulty relating to students on an individual basis and students may have more problems in forming close peer relations. One method of reducing size is to divide the student body in smaller, self-contained units.[16] Since violence is consistently higher in schools with large classes, whenever financially feasible, class size could be reduced or teachers in the junior and middle schools could be responsible for teaching in more than one subject area in order that they may work with more than one group of students for a longer period of the day.[17]

CLASSROOM MANAGEMENT AND DISCIPLINE

Lately researchers have focused not only on discipline problems within and outside of class but on classroom management, which is designed not only to improve instruction but to prevent discipline problems from arising. "Effective management," according to Evertson and Emmer, "consists of those teacher behaviors that produce high levels of student involvement in classroom activities and minimize student behaviors that interfere with the teacher's or other students' work and efficient use of instructional time."[18]

Classroom management is based on sound planning. The assumption is that sound planning and faithful execution lead to a classroom conducive to learning and few discipline problems. The first step is for teachers to be aware of their goals, belief systems, and values; in a word, their philosophy of education. Those who have not formulated a philosophy or feel incapable at present of doing so should at least try to formulate their basic goals and values about the teaching-learning process. Only in this way will they have a clear sense of direction and a source to guide them when problems and conflicts arise. Some teachers may need help in formulating their goals and values; they can be assisted in doing so through classes, workshops, outside reading, and writing assignments that provide supervised opportunities to promote thinking and articulate their ideas more fully.

The second step is to establish classroom procedures and rules and communicate them clearly to students. Rules were discussed earlier in this chapter in connection with policy; here the focus is on classroom rules essential for promoting sound instruction and preventing disruptions. Students are more likely to see the point of rules and observe them when they participate in their development. The extent to which they participate depends upon maturity, time, and feasibility. Generally more participation may be found at the secondary than at the elementary level. Time constraints and feasibility, however, require some rules to be in place at the opening of the school year; later, some rules may be cooperatively developed as a response to new problems.

It is wise to have as few rules as possible. It is better to state rules positively (what is to be done) rather than negatively (what not to do). Above all, rules need to be enforced promptly and fairly; thus teachers should not make idle threats, nor should they fail to act on infractions. Those rules that clearly contribute to educational objectives should be retained and others eliminated; no rules should violate student rights. The reasons for keeping or establishing rules should be explained so that students will be aware of their underlying purpose.

The reason for procedures is to guide student behavior in the proper performance of frequently used activities so that both classroom time will be used effectively and student competencies enhanced. Procedures include such activities as the proper handling of written asssignments in class and homework, as well as procedures governing raising questions and putting away materials at the end of the class period. Students will not only need to be thoroughly informed about procedures and checked to determine whether they understand what is expected of them, but also given an opportunity to practice the procedures under the teacher's supervision and provided prompt feedback about their performance.

Classroom activities may be divided into whole-class instruction, group work, seatwork, and individual projects. Each of these activities requires students to learn listening skills and know how to participate in an orderly and meaningful manner in discussion. Group work requires the teacher to see that other students are gainfully occupied and not causing disturbances while the teacher works with one group at a time. In assigning seatwork, each student needs to be clear about the assignment, how it is to be handled, the form it should take, the time limit involved, and whether it is permissible to collaborate with other students in completing the assigment. Individual projects need to be viewed as meaningful and worthwhile by each student, they should have a voice in the selection of the project, receive clear instructions about standards to be fulfilled, and be taught skills of independent work.

Those teachers who relate effectively to students usually have an understanding of human growth and development as well as student needs. Besides basic physical needs, students have psychosocial, emotional, and moral needs. Various psychosocial needs have been ably explained by Dreikurs (see chapter two), Maslow's hierarchy of needs,[19] and Erikson's stages of development;[20] the author has written about how to educate the emotions,[21] and the educational significance of different theories of moral development.[22] The teacher needs a sound understanding of the needs of students and how they grow and develop; this knowledge should enable the teacher to understand student behavior and to relate more effectively to them.

Learning how to learn is a characteristic found in intermediate and advanced learners. Because of the importance of such skills, it is essential that teachers systematically help students to acquire them. According to R. F. Dearden, such skills are a cluster of second-order learning skills having wide application to first-order operations.[23] Specific content learning is a first-order operation; second-order learning consists of activities such as investigating how to investigate and thinking about how to think effectively.

Learning how to learn, he claims, consists of four types of second-order skills: information-finding skills; general substantive principles (scientific principles, moral principles, or other types); formal principles of inquiry (that is methods of inquiry in the various disciplines); and self-management skills. Information-finding skills and self-management skills seem especially to be part of our concept of discipline, as a disciplined person, among other things, exhibits desirable intellectual development by completing desirable tasks and fulfilling worthwhile standards. The tasks and standards would vary according to the curriculum and the learner's level of intellectual development. Information-finding involves such learning skills as learning how to ask questions to gather needed information, learning how to listen carefully, and learning how to pay attention and to concentrate on the task at hand. One cannot complete tasks successfully or achieve goals — essential characteristics of a disciplined person — unless one has gained the rudiments of acquiring and utilizing information, listening and concentrating on the immediate tasks. Thus to teach these second-order skills and to model them for students will likely promote some of the elements of sound discipline as well as to stimulate academic achievement.

In conclusion, teachers can likely minimize everyday discipline problems by sound classroom management. This can best be accomplished by teachers understanding human growth and development; establishing clearly defined goals, rules, and procedures; and adapting procedures to the various types of classroom activities.

NOTES

1. James S. Coleman et al., *Equality of Educational Opportunity* (Washington, D.C.: Government Printing Office, 1966); and Christopher S. Jencks, *A Reassessment of Family and Schooling in America* (New York: Basic Books, 1972).
2. Brian Rowan, Steven T. Bossert, and David C. Dwyer, "Research on Effective Schools: A Cautionary Note." *Educational Researcher* 12 (1983):24.
3. Ronald R. Edmonds, "Programs of School Improvement: An Overview." *Educational Leadership* 40 (1982):4.
4. Stewart C. Purkey and Marshall S. Smith, "Too Soon to Cheer? Synthesis of Research on Effective Schools." *Educational Leadership* 40 (1982):64-69.
5. M. Rutter, B. Maughan, P. Mortimore, J. Ouston, with A. Smith, *Fifteen Thousand Hours: Secondary Schools and Their Effects on Children* (Cambridge, MA: Harvard, 1979).
6. George F. Madus, Peter W. Airasian, and Thomas Kellaghan, *School Effectiveness: A Reassessment of the Evidence* (New York: McGraw-Hill, 1980), p. 174.
7. John R. Searle, *Speech Acts* (Cambridge: University Press, 1969), pp. 33-42.
8. National Institute of Education, *Violent Schools — Safe Schools*, vol. 1 (Washington, D.C.: Department of Health, Education and Welfare, 1978), p. 3.
9. Ibid., p. 5.
10. Alfred M. Block and Ruth Reinhardt Block, "Teachers — A New Endangered Species?" In Keith Baker and Robert J. Rubel (Eds.), *Violence and Crime in the Schools* (Lexington, MA: Lexington Books, 1980), pp. 82-83.
11. National School Public Relations Association, *Vandalism and Violence: Innovative Strategies Reduce Cost to Schools* (Arlington, VA: The Association, 1971), pp. 18-39.
12. E. J. Keller, "School Security: The Role of the Police." *Law and Order* 20 (1972):50-

52.
13. E. L. Creekmore, "How Big Cities Train for School Security: A Nationwide Survey." *Security World* 11 (1974):28-29.
14. Committee on the Judiciary, *School Violence and Vandalism*. U.S. Senate, Subcommittee to Investigate Juvenile Delinquency (Washington, D.C.: Government Printing Office, 1976), p. 152.
15. Ibid., pp. 341-369.
16. Birch Bayh (Ed.), *Challenge for the Third Century: Education in a Safe Environment*. Committee on the Judiciary, U.S. Senate (Washington, D.C.: Government Printing Office, 1977), pp. 83-84.
17. NIE, *Violent Schools*, pp. 132-133.
18. Carolyn M. Evertson and Edmund T. Emmer, "Preventive Classroom Management." In Daniel L. Duke (Ed.), *Helping Teachers Manage Classrooms* (Alexandia, VA: Association for Supervision and Curriculum Development, 1982), p. 6.
19. A. H. Maslow, *Motivation and Personality* (New York: Harper & Row, 1954).
20. Eric Erikson, *Childhood and Society*, 2nd. ed. (New York: Norton, 1963).
21. John Martin Rich, "On Educating the Emotions." *Educational Theory* 27 (1977):291-296.
22. John Martin Rich and Joseph L. DeVitis, *Theories of Moral Development* (Springfield, IL: Thomas, 1985).
23. R. F. Dearden, *Problems in Primary Education* (London: Routledge & Kegan Paul, 1976), pp. 69-74.

Chapter Six

A NORMATIVE PROACTIVE
THEORY OF DISCIPLINE

THIS CHAPTER presents my own normative proactive theory of discipline as an alternative to views considered earlier in the book, not only the models in chapter two but also the historical models in chapter one. Of course my theory has been influenced by the works of others but seeks to provide a coherent and intelligible explanation of disciplinary phenomena in its own terms. The theoretical and philosophical grounds of my position will be briefly presented and their implications for educational policy and practice will be indicated.

First, the nature of discipline will be explored and the meaning of the terms "normative" and "proactive" will be clarified. Next, it will be shown that discipline has a special relationship to authority and that authority has a number of significant forms that shape discipline in different ways. Third, teacher-student relations will be explored in terms of what dehumanizes the relationship; the applicable humanistic principles will be presented and their significance shown. Finally, some questions arise as to how best to motivate students in light of these principles and whether it would be acceptable to use rewards and punishment.

THE NATURE OF DISCIPLINE

What is meant by a normative proactive theory of discipline? The *normative* aspects of discipline refer to the moral grounds on which discipline could be based. These moral grounds will be explicated later in the chapter when teacher-student relations are discussed.

Discipline is active rather than passive. It is not something done to someone; it is *proactive* rather than passive or reactive. The person is the doer of the action: it may involve physical movement, ranging from usual functioning to vigorous and quickened action. Agency for action is of primary importance. Agency is attributed to people and partly to animals, not things or events.

Is it then accurate to say that someone was disciplined for misbehavior if discipline is active and therefore not something done to someone else? Here punishment and disapproval is to impose sanctions for misbehavior that fails to meet approved standards. What is done to get students to observe the standards is not discipline itself but certain external devices used to promote discipline by encouraging students to initiate better behavior.

Discipline is goal directed. As long as the goals are compelling motives for participating and give a reason for action, it is accurate to say that it is goal directed. The goals of discipline are diverse because they depend upon the purposes for which discipline is undertaken. Such goals can be divided into extrinsic and intrinsic ones. Extrinsic goals could include: perform a task, demonstrate the ability to follow instructions, and to learn to comply with deadlines. Intrinsic goals, in contrast, are about a well-disciplined person who manifests a certain type of character or intellectual disposition because of internal values rather than external requirements (as in the case of extrinsic goals).

That an activity is goal directed does not in itself make it desirable: it is necessary to examine the desirability of the goals themselves and also look at the means used to attain the goals. Those means or instrumentalities that do not respect the student's intellectual integrity and are dehumanizing are unacceptable.

Discipline may take the form of individual, group, or team arrangements. The team may be found in sports, games, life-saving teams, and the like. Discipline in school is usually an individual or group matter. The classroom itself may be viewed as a group and the teacher a group leader who uses group dynamics. Problems become individual rather than group when a student chooses to act in violation of legitimate disciplinary rules. It becomes a group problem whenever students deliberately act conjointly and whose results violate rules.

Discipline features constitutive rules as well as regulative rules governing performance of learning tasks. Constitutive rules would be found in academic subjects; and to the extent that students need to learn the rules in order to master the subject could be an instance in which discipline comes into play.

To the extent that standards are present and observed in activities, school discipline is largely refereed. By *refereed* is meant that some authority figure is present to see that the standards are fulfilled according to acceptable procedures. Penalties may be imposed when standards are not fulfilled or are deliberately violated. Penalties, in the form of various sanctions, are imposed to gain compliance with rules and standards; the penalties, however, are not discipline per se but external devices designed to promote discipline or restore a lapse from sound disciplinary behavior. Sanctions and other external devices cannot in themselves discipline without gaining the cooperation of students; otherwise, there would be no student agency and therefore no discipline, although there may be coercion and consequently control.

But why do discipline problems arise? If discipline is required to gain a certain level of mastery of a subject and the student lacks the requisite discipline, then the desired level of mastery cannot be attained. Thus it is necessary for the teacher to recognize the present abilities of students and to set tasks that can be mastered by allowing as much time as feasible for sufficient practice opportunities in acquiring new competencies.

Some students lack adequate motivation and self-control. They see little point in their studies and consequently have difficulty concentrating and applying themselves; and their lack of self-control dissipates their energies and impulses in directions that oppose disciplinary goals.

Students who belong to groups or cliques may fail to observe rules because they are following their peers. The clique's goals may differ from instructional goals; and where the student follows the clique's goals by choice rather than coercion, it would fit into our theory of discipline.

Adverse environmental conditions may contribute to disciplinary problems: excessive noise, overcrowding, improperly ventilated rooms, and unsafe playgrounds and hallways. Thus it behooves teachers and administrators to see to it that a healthy and safe learning environment is maintained.

AUTHORITY AND DISCIPLINE

Authority is the framewok in which discipline rests. Authority presupposes a normative order not only in which one can appeal in cases of dispute over rules and laws but one where social life takes place and models for codes of conduct are approved.

According to Thomas Hobbes, men in a state of nature, although approximately equal in strength, mental capacity, and experience, continue to exploit one another until a state of war ensues. Thus life would be "solitary, poor, nasty, brutish and short." Hobbes' solution for overcoming this precarious, warring state is for each person, when others are also willing to do so, to lay down his right to all things and to be content with as much liberty toward others as others have against himself. This is made possible by each person relinquishing his or her right and vesting it in a sovereign who in turn has the authority to establish laws and impose sanctions for their violation.

Thus there can be no genuine discipline without growing up in a culture that conveys a normative order in which authority figures — parents, teachers, judges, and the like — inculcate expected ways of behavior that consist of mores, folkways, laws, and other norms. It is the authority figure who embodies the norms, models and inculcates them variously and imposes sanctions when norms are violated.

Authority has been associated with force and coercion; however, although authority figures may resort to their use, there are other ways that authority is exercised. A distinction can be made between force and coercion. Coerced persons become the tool of another; they still have the choice, under the constraint, of choosing the least undesirable course of action. Although laws can be viewed as coercive, one still has the choice of disobeying the law. In contrast when subjected to force, one does not act but is acted upon; certain things are done to the individual. Thus when persons are forced, they can be excused because they do not act and therefore cannot be held responsible; whereas one can be held partly responsible for acts performed under coercion depending upon the circumstances of the case.

A person in authority usually has the capacity to coerce; it is the capacity itself rather than actual coercion that may render an authority effective. Authority carries with it certain symbols surrounding the prestige, traditions, and ceremonies of the office. (Consider the symbols surrounding the office of a monarch.) Some tacit symbols surround the potential power and coerciveness that the office holder exercises, and the recognition that they could be used is usually sufficient to discourage wrongdoing. Thus whenever coercion is frequently resorted to there is an indication that authority is insufficiently respected and the symbols of office do not regulate effectively. Coercive potential varies with the office: principals have more of this potential than teachers, superintendents more than principals. Generally, during the 1970s the teacher's tacit symbols were less effective in regulating than in earlier periods and some teachers had to use considerable coercion to restore order. Despite the fact that authority is probably more effective when coercion is not used, it is not an abuse of authority unless the coercive practices violate student rights or school regulations.

Power is a more encompassing term than either coercion or force. Power is the ability to get someone to carry out one's will despite resistance on their part. Thus *A* has power over *B* if *B* resists *A* but still acts in the way *A* prescribes. Power may take the form of participating in the decision-making of others. Where the use of coercion or force is successful, it would be a form of power. In other words, power has a success or achievement dimension, whereas one cannot unsuccessfully attempt to coerce or use force and call it power. But power may also be used in behavior modification, conditioning, hypnosis, and other devices; it is said to be an example of power when the subject is rendered incapable of resistance.

Power is closely related to *influence*. The influential person sways, affects, or alters another by indirect or intangible means, either consciously or unconsciously. In contrast, power is usually direct, conscious, and tangible; moreover, the power wielder can invoke sanctions but the influential person cannot do so. The media star influences innumerable fans to buy his records and cassettes without using sanctions; the appeal may be intangible or ineffable (especially to outside onlookers who fail to be swayed by the media star's presence).

Do teachers have much power and, if they do, are they generally permitted to use it? Teachers as well as administrators have found their power limited in recent years as a consequence of court decisions surrounding student due process rights, corporal punishment, dress codes, and the like. Teachers, however, do exercise power where laws permit them to use corporal punishment (even under circumscribed conditions) and other forms of physical control over recalcitrant students. It should be remembered that teachers need the use of sanctions and the application of power should achieve its objectives to make a warranted claim about power in any given situation. Teachers may have authority to require students to remain after school for various reasons; but if students do not comply with the teacher's demand, then it could be said that the teacher does not have actual power in this situation. To the extent that teachers overcome student resistance by techniques of behavior modification and conditioning, then power is being exercised whenever sanctions can be applied. For the most part, however, the conception of power described above is a characteristic of key administrators, legislators, judges, and law enforcement officials. Of course all of these persons have restrictions on their activities by having the spheres of their power defined and delimited by statutes or official policy.

It might be said that teachers exercise authority more by influence than power. But some forms of influence are based on charisma and most teachers lack charisma. Influence, on the other hand, may take the form of symbols embodied in the office of teacher. Teachers may give orders and expect students to obey them; the legitimacy of teachers doing so rests upon their office and the expectation that teachers will enforce school and class-room rules. But some students, for whatever reasons, do not respect the teacher's office and therefore the tacit symbols do not serve to regulate.

Teachers have other devices, however, when the symbols of the office prove ineffectual. Teachers can appeal to their expertise. The notion of expertise is usually that of appealing to an authority in one circumscribed area of competence and assessing, if not always utilizing, the competence of the authority. The teacher's claim to expertise would rest upon knowledge of pedagogy and the discipline taught. The young child is in a vulnerable position and must take on face-value the pronouncements of parents and teachers; but usually by the early teens, some youth begin to find their peers a better guide than the seemingly antiquated ideas of parents and teachers. Unless teachers can arouse student interest in the subject, appeal to expertise will likely be ineffectual.

The teacher may also serve as a model. Even though a student may not choose teaching as a career, the teacher can be a model of desirable traits to emulate. A model is something or someone held up for purposes of guidance or imitation, and a person may be considered a standard of excellence to be imitated. The model must be a significant person in the eyes of the observer; and the observer needs to be attentive to what the model does and have the ability to perform the modeled act. This is an effective way to handle discipline because the teacher is modeling desirable behavior rather than being coercive. Although more teachers likely serve as a model than exercise charisma, it is unlikely that the teacher can be a model to every student in class; consequently, other devices must be employed.

When teachers are unable to serve as a model to certain students, and if the students do not respect the office of teacher, they may respect the teacher's expertise; and if they lack respect for expertise, they may respect or, more likely, fear negative sanctions. It is better, however, for the teacher to attempt to establish trust and good will and try to humanize interpersonal relations in the classroom.

HUMANISTIC TEACHER-STUDENT RELATIONS

In order to develop humanistic teacher-student relations, it is first necessary to understand the impediments to such relations—most notably, the characteristics of dehumanizing conditions. What is dehumanization? The concept has both an inward as well as an outward dimension. The outward dimension is the interpersonal relations by which people relate to one another. The inward dimension can be observed in the way a relationship makes a person feel and how it affects his or her self-concept and sense of personal dignity. The latter dimension can be observed in facial expressions, voice tone, body posture and expression, and other outward manifestations of emotions. There are certain paradigm cases that can be used to determine a dehumanizing situation; some of these paradigms may be more applicable to Western, than non-Western, cultures. Recalling that dehumanization occurs when an event or interpersonal relation is perceived by the individual as an attack on or threat to one's self-concept or a significant loss or damage to one's personal dignity, then it can be understood why certain outcomes will likely be dehumanizing.

Any interpersonal relationship that has one or more of the following effects on the individual is dehumanizing: (1) brutalization, (2) humiliation in terms of one's sense of dignity, (3) a situation that causes a partial loss or aggravation of one's sense of identity, (4) a situation wherein one perceives him or herself as treated as a thing, object, or piece of property to be manipulated rather than a person to be respected, and (5) a situation that causes individuals to feel that they are not in control of their actions, but that the actions are caused by known or unseen forces which cannot be resisted.

It is not always easy to remove the conditions that dehumanize because teachers and administrators do not always recognize the conditions. Some conditions may be present in large, impersonal bureaucratic school systems that elevate efficiency higher than sound human relations. Other contributing factors are such commonplace features as the grading system. While not implying that grades always have a deleterious effect on students, the undesirable effects that they do have should be mentioned. Schools make the failure of one child the success of another. The pressure to make good grades can cause students to cheat, to become anxious and apprehensive, to consider themselves failures, to refuse to help their classmates, and to contemplate — and in some cases to commit — suicide. Of various solutions proposed, one would be to substitute for the traditional grading system various flexible systems of evaluation experimented with during the early progressive movement. Another is to see how alternative schools are handling evaluation and to adopt whatever practices found there that would appear to be workable. Finally, more teachers could use a master learning approach that assumes that 90-95% of students can master a subject if given sufficient time and are provided instruction matched to their needs and style of learning.

But it is not enough to eliminate conditions that dehumanize; it is also necesary to adopt humanistic principles and practices. Kant wanted humankind to observe a categorical imperative or practical moral law that holds in all social and moral relations. Rational beings, he claimed, exist as ends in themselves, not merely as a means to be used by others. Rational beings are persons and, since persons are ends in themselves, no person can be substituted for another, for if this was the case no person would have absolute worth. By permitting substitution the categorical imperative would become conditional and no longer serve as a practical moral law of human relations. Thus it is, for Kant, to treat humanity, both oneself and others, in every case as an end and never as a means only.

My own conception of respect for persons is to exhibit esteem or honor for the person, or to show consideration or concern. But if it is said that we should show respect for others just because they are persons, then in many cases we may not show honor or esteem but just consideration (which should be sufficient and it is all the principle demands). Yet we do this because either they are persons like ourselves or we prize the traits of being a person. The notion of being a person is a normative concept insofar as being a person is to exhibit such valued traits as rationality, aesthetic sensitivity, refined emotions, moral agency, free will, and the like. Whether these or some other traits are ascribed to persons, it does pose problems as to how human beings who are deficient in some of these traits ought to be treated.

Even those with deficient traits should not be inflicted with avoidable pain, harm or suffering; one should see that all persons, whether normal or deficient, are afforded the protection of just rules and laws. Respecting persons may also mean that societies should make provision for universal education at public expense and support a legal system that safeguards basic rights.

Educators are more likely to relate humanistically to students by using an ideographic holistic approach. This approach is an attempt to relate to students as unique beings and to understand them as total persons. One comes to recognize other persons as beings in their own right with their own present actualities and future possibilities.

A way of thinking that seeks to know from the inside is similar to *verstehen*. Thus an attempt is made to study not merely what people do, but the thoughts, value judgments, and purposes which have led them to do it. Our knowledge is not limited to the phenomenal and external.

One can understand in terms of the motive of the actor performing an act. We understand why someone fires a gun when we know the actor's motive for doing so. By like token, when a person who is walking at a normal pace suddenly breaks into a run, the reason for the act is not evident from the behavior. Sudden fear, lateness for an appointment, the desire for exercise, or some other motive may be the causal factor. The observer has to comprehend the relationship between the motives and the overt behavior. One may look for typical patterns of motives in typical situations.

While not denying the reality of scientific behavioral thinking, idiographic holistic thinking refuses to accept its results as final; nor does it accept the claim that the extension of scientific methods from the natural sciences to the study of human behavior is in itself sufficient to provide the knowledge we seek. Scientific behavioral research seeks to discover uniformities and regularities characteristic of a whole class of objects. Idiographic holistic approach attempts to reveal the particular pattern in a unique individual, to understand the individual as a unique being rather than as a specimen of a class.

How can educators best use this approach? Observed factors in a situation are understandable by applying generalizations based on experience. Generalizations are developed over many years through self-observation and introspection. Why someone becomes angry can be understood by applying generalizations from our experience that are pertinent to situations of the type in which the anger occurs.

But this procedure has inherent limitations which require that it be supplemented by other procedures. The approach overly relies upon the richness and depth of individual personal experience and the perceptiveness and insight acquired by means of these experiences. As such, the procedure would limit use of the idiographic holistic approach to those educators who have excelled in refining the meaning of their experience.

Initially we begin to know other people by getting them to tell us about themselves. Still, we need to get to know them more from "the inside," and this can likely be accomplished by understanding their values, aims, and aspirations. Why a person makes sacrifices for others, perseveres in the face of great hardships, and works diligently without certainty of reward can be explained in terms of values, aims, and motives. Similarly, why a student rebels, refuses to follow a teacher's instructions, or chooses to drop out of school can can also be understood by the same approach.

Empathy is another important feature that promotes a view from the inside. The teacher attempts to understand the ideas, value system, and cultural background that influence the students' actions. The teacher should try to grasp the basic value systems of the culture (as represented by the students in class). In other words, empathy aids the teacher in comprehending the panoply of ideas, values, and aspirations that are expressed and underlie actions, whether shared or unique.

By understanding others in this manner, teachers are in a better position to help students to continue to grow and to help them transcend their present circumstances and self-imposed limitations. These tasks can be accomplished by integrating new experiences and ideas that enable students to gain greater self-mastery and assume increased responsibility for their own education. The teacher's ability to understand the student's perceptions does not mean that the teacher has the same reaction as the student; it means instead that the teacher can understand why the student is disturbed, perplexed, or joyful. The teacher strives not only to gain an understanding of students' thoughts and feelings and their ways of relating to others but also seeks to inspire students to be themselves and to become the best selves of which they are capable. Teachers who are able to accomplish these tasks not only use idiographic holistic thinking but genuinely care about students and have courage to face a largely indifferent world and their own negation (death). This means that teachers must first care for and respect themselves, that they need to make themselves whole before they can fruitfully use an idiographic holistic approach; only in this way is it possible genuinely to care about others so that they can become the best selves of which they are capable.

MOTIVATION, RULES, AND PUNISHMENT

Should teachers seek to motivate students through rewards and punishment? Of the models presented in chapter two, Dreikurs' ideas on this topic appear to be the most sound. As you may recall, he substituted natural and logical consequences for rewards and punishment and held that it is better to offer students encouragement while they pursue a learning activity rather than providing rewards after completing the task successfully. Although natural and logical consequences are useful conceptual distinctions, the problem is whether these distinctions hold up in practice or become confused with rewards and punishment.

Students need to be actively involved in pursuing learning tasks and assume increasingly greater responsibility for their classroom activities. But to be involved means to be motivated — and it is preferable, if self-discipline is to be cultivated, that motivation should not be based primarily on rewards and punishment. Students may be involved in learning tasks because doing so would likely lead to something worthwhile (as learning mathematics to help one in business transactions) or desirable for its own sake (working math problems viewed as an enjoyable pastime). Rewards are not likely to develop desirable discipline because they may have a coercive effect, deny self-agency and, when withdrawn, the behavior usually collapses. Better, as Dreikurs suggests, to give encouragement on the task. Also, when students see what they are studying is meaningful, that it has some bearing on either their present or future concerns, then they are likely to become more involved and take greater responsiblity for their learning.

Although Dreikurs' natural and logical consequences are useful conceptual distinctions and could prove valuable if they can be demarcated in practice from rewards and punishment, my approach to punishment differs from Dreikurs' model and perhaps many of the other models studied in chapter two.

Teachers can use *nonphysical* punishment effectively and avoid many dangerous pitfalls by observing certain important conditions and practices. Although still legally permissible and commonplace in American schools, corporal punishment is a special case with its own problems and is more difficult to justify than other forms of punishment; therefore the focus will be on nonphysical punishment.

It is first necessary to distinguish among punishment, control, and discipline. Punishment involves unpleasantness or the infliction of pain by someone in authority as a consequence of violating rules. Thus, a perceptual element is found in punishment: Not only must the teacher define the punishment as a penalty for rule infraction, but the student must also perceive it as punishment.

Punishment can be imposed only by those in authority because they are authorized to do so. Teachers can administer punishment as long as it is in keeping with school policy, but one student cannot punish another; parents can punish their children, but neighbors cannot do so unless the parent authorizes it. Thus punishment is a quasi-legal notion, whereas one student who inflicts pain on another may be committing an act of aggression, violence or assault and battery.

Punishment seems to contribute more directly to control than to discipline. Control is found where there is sufficient order in the classroom for teachers to conduct planned activities without undue interference or disruption. Thus, as can be seen from our earlier discussion of the nature of discipline, control and discipline are separate and distinct; however, control may be a necessary condition for desired disciplinary dispositions to develop.

Punishment, in certain cases, may help to restore order; it may contribute to rudimentary discipline training by teaching students to obey rules and follow instructions. However, since there may be more desirable practices for developing such traits, punishment would have to be weighed against alternatives. Yet, when rules are violated, whether or not doing so leads to classroom disruption, it seems logical, under certain conditions, to impose punishment.

Since punishment cannot be imposed except when rules are violated, it is important that the conditions about the use of rules, as mentioned in chapter five, be observed: Rules should not violate student rights; students, whenever feasible, should participate in formulating rules; keep the rules few in number and state them positively and clearly; and enforce rules promptly, firmly, and fairly. It is usually not necessary to single out each rule for justification — only those contested or frequently not observed; it is usually sufficient to provide an overall rationale for classroom policy.

In using punishment, teachers should avoid inculcating feelings of failure and inadequacy. One way to do this is to have students understand classroom rules and to participate in their formulation. Additionally, it should be clear to the student that a specific behavior is being punished. The rule violation and the subsequent punishment should not be separate in space and time so that the connection between the two is unclear.

In fact, punishment is more effective at the beginning of the act than after it is completed, and the longer one waits to punish, the less effective the punishment. Thus, it may be best to wait until the student begins to repeat the behavior before administering punishment. Where punishment is delayed, it is important that the student clearly understand what rule has been violated before being punished.

Punishment should not be harsh or excessive. Teachers who punish in fits of anger or resentment are likely to succumb to such temptations; thus, punishment needs to be administered calmly and deliberately and as briefly and mildly as the infraction and situation permit. It is desirable to combine punishment with positive statements of expectations which point out what the offender should be doing rather than what he or she should not do. While the undesirable behavior is weakened, it is important to teach correct behavior.

Once more positive measures have been tried and persistent misbehavior leaves no alternative, punishment can be used without causing resentment, anxiety, or a sense of failure if the teacher shows genuine care and respect for students and for safeguarding their rights. One way the teacher shows respect for persons is to expect students to fulfill their potentials and to take full advantage of available learning opportunities.

APPENDIX

SCHOOL DISCIPLINE IMPROVEMENT SURVEY

1. Has you school developed a student handbook of rights and responsibilities?

     YES   NO

   If the answer is YES, indicate how these rules were developed:

   ___ By the administration   ___ With parent involvement
   ___ By administrators and teachers ___ With student involvement

   If the answer to Number 1 is NO, is responsibility for classroom disciplinary rules left to each teacher?

     YES   NO

   If the answer is NO, please describe briefly how disciplinary rules are handled.

2. Does your school have a special program for handling difficult disciplinary problems?

     YES   NO

   If the answer is YES, who is in charge of the program?

   ___ Principal and administrative   ___ Designated teacher
       staff   Other _____
   ___ Principal
   ___ Guidance counselor

3. Which model below would best describe your special program?

   ___ Behavior Modification   ___ Gordon's Teacher
   ___ Canter's Assertive Model   Effectiveness Training
   ___ Dreikurs' Social Discipline Model ___ Redl and Wattenberg Group
   ___ Engelmann and Dobson   Management
       Behavior/Punishment Model   ___ Rich's Normative Proactive
   ___ Giott's Communication Model   Discipline
   ___ Glasser's Reality Model   ___ Transactional Analysis
                                       ___ Values Clarification
                                       OTHER _____

4. List briefly what you believe to be three primary causes of everyday classroom discipline problems.

   (1)

(2)

(3)

5. Please place a check mark below in those areas where your school has developed written policies or rules regulating student behavior:

___ Attendance

___ Due process

___ Interrogation

___ Detention

___ Suspension and expulsion

___ Dress code

___ Student records

___ Coordination of discipline action with guidance and counseling

___ Student grievance procedures

___ Student disciplinary committee

___ Student participation in developing school rules

___ Regulation of student records

___ Corporal punishment

___ Vandalism and/or theft

___ Search and seizure for illegal items

___ Parent-teacher & parent-administrator discipline conferences

___ Law enforcement officers in the school

___ Alcohol

___ Parental liability for their children's vandalism

___ Smoking and tobacco

___ Drugs

___ Gambling

___ Profanity and abusive language

___ Extortion/intimidation

___ Forgery

___ Cheating

___ Misdemeanors/felonies

___ Trespassing

___ Bomb threats

___ Physical assault on school personnel

___ Physical assaults on students

___ Fighting

Others _____

_____

Name of Respondent: _____

Position: _____

School: _____

Address: _____

_____

_____

Telephone: _____

INDEX